BROKEN PIE CHART

5 Ways to Build Your
Investment Portfolio to
Withstand and Prosper in
Risky Markets

BROKEN PIE CHART

5 Ways to Build Your Investment Portfolio to Withstand and Prosper in Risky Markets

BY

DEREK MOORE
Razor Wealth Management LLC, Scottsdale, AZ, USA

United Kingdom — North America — Japan
India — Malaysia — China

Emerald Publishing Limited
Howard House, Wagon Lane, Bingley BD16 1WA, UK

First edition 2018

British Library Cataloguing in Publication Data
A catalogue record for this book is available from the British Library

ISBN: 978-1-78743-554-4 (Print)
ISBN: 978-1-78743-553-7 (Online)
ISBN: 978-1-78743-958-0 (Epub)

ISOQAR certified
Management System,
awarded to Emerald
for adherence to
Environmental
standard
ISO 14001:2004.

Certificate Number 1985
ISO 14001

INVESTOR IN PEOPLE

For Kelly and Jackson

CONTENTS

ACKNOWLEDGMENTS

First, I wanted to thank my family for the support during the writing of this book, which took many nights and weekends. Thank you, Kelly and Jackson!

Special thanks to my agent Jeanne Levine, who was tremendous to work with and helped bring this project from the initial proposal all the way through.

I also can't leave out the team at ZEGA Financial LLC including Jay Pestrichelli, Wayne Ferbert, Mick Brokaw, and Jillian Baker.

Thanks to Charlotte Maiorana, Senior Editor at Emerald Publishing Limited, for believing in the project immediately.

Finally, thank you to my parents who read so many books to me at an early age I was bound to write one of my own one day.

PREFACE: DID 2008 TEACH US ANYTHING?

Leading into the 2008 Great Recession most investors had some form of a traditional asset allocation. The usual mix of stocks and bonds that could graphically be shown in a nicely created pie chart on statements. Many were surprised to find out it did little to insulate them from a severe drawdown in their assets. You would think things would have changed? There would be mass adoption of using new methods to construct portfolios? Sadly, I see more of the same approach.

While investment pie charts may be broken for our current markets, I didn't see much in the way of discussion in the media on the subject. My motivation in writing this book was to highlight why traditional asset allocations may fail in the coming decades. Too often annualized historical returns are quoted from many years of past performance. Unfortunately, most individuals have windows of opportunity that might span only 10, 15, or 20 years. Will the prime investing years realize the average or something worse? What happens if markets have sharp corrections? What if markets are stagnant offering little cumulative returns?

In the coming chapters, we will examine why traditional portfolios may not be your best chance at success in the coming decades. We'll also investigate the potential for bonds to have a lost decade or two leading to little real returns. Instead, new asset classes will be discussed to modernize your investment pie chart. One of the goals in writing this book is to increase all your probabilities for maximizing your assets into retirement and have the ability in retirement to support the lifestyle you hoped for.

These days we see more and more concentration into broad exchange traded funds. We have Central Banks around the world with record levels of assets on the balance sheets. The Federal Reserve may or may not be successful at winding down their balance sheet. Interest rates have been the lowest in over 500 years in many parts of the world. This distortion in keeping rates low has caused future earnings to be discounted down barely with such low rates.

When we examine all the debt countries around the world are racking up, it is staggering to think what their interest payments on the debt will become if rates should rise. Even at the current low interest rates, debt continues to grow to levels that would make it hard to believe could ever be contained.

If you look at the economy, while unemployment statistics are approaching full employment by historical yard sticks, real wages have not really grown much since the 2008 recession. All of the additions to the money supply might eventually lead to inflation or maybe growth will stay in the "low growth" environment some point to.

With low rates, where investors don't earn much in traditional bonds, those approaching retirement using classical asset allocations might not earn a real return above inflation in the next decade. Or worst case, rates spike and all those bond funds see significant losses in their market values.

When we look at how success is measured we continue to hear about how a 60/40 portfolio has performed or how some blend of stocks and bonds over long periods of time have provided really nice average annual returns. Yet if an investor only has 10 years to retirement why chance not getting the average? Considering there have been long periods of relatively flat returns with corrections build in, wouldn't it make sense to seek out new approaches and alternatives? Too often retirement savers still need growth but can't afford to take on the downside risk of equities with no downside protection.

Speaking of downside, all too often investment performance ratios that are based on using the standard deviation or volatility of past years might miss out on what is truly important to someone who has specific goals. More and more though we continue to see investors and retirement savings boxed into some asset allocation based upon not what they need but simply how old they are. Sometimes those investments are misunderstood and unfortunately the true downside risk inherent in the underlying makeup of the investments.

As we move forward there needs to be consideration for the number of years an investor has until events like retirement. The idea of using a risk tolerance and age to build a portfolio with assumptions for forward returns based upon at times over 100 years of historical returns may be setting up people to fail. For many years, the mix of equities and bonds seemed to balance out risk. On the equity side, you shot for growth while bonds paid out a nice annual rate of interest. Those interest payments made forgoing growth on that portion of the pie chart palpable as the cost to carry fixed income was not that great.

As we will find rates falling from the highs of 1981 for the next 35 years cause outsized returns in many years for bond funds. If rates stay low, there is very little to be gained by just collecting interest payments that may only beat inflation by a tiny bit. If rates do rise they threaten to mimic the hit to market values of the 1970s albeit with less margin for error since unlike that period coupon rate payments will not be in the double digits.

Portfolios need to be built with the time frame of peak effect on assets. Someone with 5 years but needing growth to spur retirement income may not want to just use the same old age-based asset allocation. Many investors have a 10- to 15-year window to maximize returns. Relying on their window being within a great bull market isn't enough. What if markets suffer from a sideways market over years? What if there are significant pullbacks like in the early 2000s and 2008–2009?

The good news is there are new updated pie charts available if you know where to look. With the advances made utilizing options strategies can build in hedges and buffers to risk. Portfolios can contain strategies that look to sell outsized volatility premium in the markets. Unfortunately, many portfolio choices available in 401k's are just a mix and match of the standard classical asset classes.

Portfolios are still constructed using methods dating back to 1950s and 1960s yet we don't use the same phones. We don't drive the same cars. Respectfully I would ask, why are we using the same asset allocations? If we are setting up for a period of very low bond yields and lower growth, allocations should be modernized.

1

WHAT'S IN YOUR PIE CHART?

On most investment prospectus or disclaimers, it usually says past performance is no indication of future success. Yet in looking to build portfolios that produce the best returns with the least risk, most do use past historical performance to create a framework for classical portfolios. For many years, investors have built portfolios owning some mix of stocks and bonds. Often, they are printed out in a nice graphical pie chart to illustrate the percent allocated to each. The most aggressive of investors would slant toward 100% stocks, while a conservative or income-seeking individual might be almost 100% in bonds. It would be natural to gravitate toward some mix to reduce annualized portfolio volatility, especially as one gets to retirement age.

Portfolios are then named after their makeup of assets. Many will point to historical returns over long periods, as evidence that what worked in the past will continue to work going forward. A keep-it-simple approach might suggest subtracting one's current age from 100 to figure out what percentage can be in stocks. Someone who is 40 years of age using that formula would do simple math and come up with a 60/40 stocks/bonds mix. A statement might include a pie chart as shown in Figure 1.

Yet will this approach work in the next decade or two? You see often historical returns are given that represent many years. Some go back to the late 1800s. Bond returns such as long, intermediate,

1

Figure 1. Classic 60% Stocks and 40% Bonds Allocation.

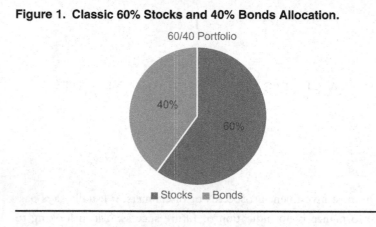

60/40 Portfolio

40%

60%

▪ Stocks ▪ Bonds

Table 1. Average Annual Returns 1928–2016 with Standard Deviation and Range.

	S&P 500 Total Return (%)	10-Year Treasury Total Return (%)
Average annual return	11.42	5.18
Standard deviation	19.59	7.72
1-Standard deviation range	−8.17 to +31.01	−2.54 to +12.90
2-Standard deviation range	−27.76 to +50.60	−10.26 to +20.62

Data Source: Aswath Damodaran NYU Stern School of Business.

---

and short-term treasuries include periods that are historically bullish with higher interest rates spanning multiple decades. If you use enough years, it smooths out the shorter run bumps in returns when markets correct. If we use a total return as in Table 1 we can see between 1928 and 2016, the S&P 500 and Treasury 10-Year Bond's continuous maturity.

1.1. HISTORICAL RETURN AVERAGES

All of this is fine, but will investors get the historical averages or something different going forward? You see the problem is many individuals only have segments of time to achieve their goals. Markets have had periods where selloffs happen even multiple times. Other times may just have next to nothing in cumulative growth over a decade or more — a so-called lost decade for investors. Bonds, as we will learn later, are using historical numbers whose replication moving forward in the next 10–20 years is doubtful.

1.2. LIFECYCLE FOR INVESTORS

Investors are often thought of as being in various stages of their investment life. You've probably heard these cycles referred to as accumulation, preservation, and distribution. Accumulation deals with the period when investors are building their accounts and contributing assets. Including those able to put extra funds away in taxable accounts and participate in a company's 401k plan. Inherently contributing to company retirement plans allows each paycheck to dollar cost average into investments.

Preservation is next where the goal is to grow a little bit but de-risk portfolios to look to manage for less volatility and downside. I view this stage a little different though. As we will see later, adding new pieces to the pie chart may allow for potential returns in various market conditions while allowing for more market exposure while hedging the downside. This is a crucial period, as by now investors have a base of assets to work with. What many call preservation, I would call base maximization. This is a crucial stage where catastrophic downturns or periods of no or low returns can derail the ability to retire and the quality of life thereafter. Really, 15 years to retirement period is where many can advance their balances. The goal should be protecting but look to surge the value of portfolios. The problem is what will typical markets like stocks and bonds deliver during this period?

Finally, the distribution phase where drawdowns from portfolios will be needed to fund income needs. This is equally important. When we think about drawdowns, we refer to withdrawing money on a periodic basis to use for income, now that one isn't drawing the same salary any longer. The ability for assets to last is a function of the return on assets post retirement, the rate of inflation, and the amount taken out. It used to be a no brainer to transition to a portfolio of mostly bonds. Yet as we will discuss, the time for new entries into our pie chart has come. Alternatives to the classic allocations are needed as bonds are likely to offer little total return in the next decade.

1.3. INVESTORS MAY NOT REALIZE THE AVERAGE OF SHORTER TIME PERIODS

Because investors have limited amounts of time to get what they need out of the various markets, it will be important to modernize their portfolios. People don't have 100 years to realize the averages. They have real goals and aspirations. They want to be able to return and support a lifestyle. Some polls (Gallup, 2014) indicated an average of 69% of people aged 30–64 worried about not having enough money for retirement. While stocks over time have produced some of the best annualized returns for investors, they also have had periods of significant downturns.

Stocks have also had periods of unbelievable runs. At the same time, they have experienced lost decades. If one is in that maximization period and stocks have a magical run of significant returns, those fears of retirement might go away or at least be significantly improved. Stocks returns in each year are a combination of their change in market value and dividends paid to form a total return. This doesn't account for capital gains tax paid in the case of nonqualified accounts. We can also look at a simple point-to-point cumulative return in an underlying index like the Dow Jones to identify periods of both little growth or stagnation and periods of powerful secular bull markets. When markets offer small or negative cumulative returns, all investors are left with are the dividends. Cumulative returns simply are a point-to-point percentage gain or loss excluding dividends. If we look at some historical periods in the Dow Jones Industrial Index in Table 2, we see a great disparity in segments of time in the markets.

This data should be stunning to some. It's hard to imagine 25 years, point to point, of essentially nothing to show for equity investments but dividends as happened between 1929 and 1954. More recently, the 2000–2010 decade was one of no growth. Then you have the end of 1982 to the end of the 1999, when stocks cumulative return was over 1000%. This is exactly the reason stocks must be part of a portfolio simply because they offer the opportunity to have runs like this. Part of designing portfolios with equity strategies that offer downside protection is if markets do run great. If they don't, there is other "stuff" in there to try to produce and carry the weight.

Table 2. Dow Jones Industrial Index Cumulative Return.

Period	Length (Years)	Cumulative Return (%)
1/1897–1/1906	9	+148.92
2/1906–6/1924	18	−4.29
7/1924–8/1929	5	+294.66
9/1929–11/1954	25	+1.69
12/1954–1/1966	11	+154.29
2/1966–10/1982	17	+0.83
11/1982–12/1999	17	+1059.31
1/2000–12/2010	11	+0.70
1/2011–12/2016	6?	+70.70

Data Source: Guggenheim Investments.

Japan's Nikkei 224 Index provides an even starker illustration of how point-to-point cumulative index returns may suffer through periods of no growth. Now Japan has its own set of issues as they have been stuck in a low growth, low-interest rate environment since the height of their economy in the late eighties. But if we look at the historical Nikkei 225 monthly returns since 1983 in Figure 2, we can see there has been little growth since that markets run up.

That's not to say there have not been buying opportunities in the early 2000s and post Great Recession. But this market has not offered very high real cumulative returns over vast periods.

Similar to our Dow Jones table on cumulative returns over cyclical market periods, the Nikkei 224 Index had a powerful bull market up to the end of 1989 but periods of negative and flat point to point returns excluding dividends (Table 3).

While it may be easy to explain away the Japanese stock market as dissimilar to those in Europe and the United States, they experienced a large rise in share prices, but to this day have never recovered to the previous heights. The chart of the Nikkei 225 Index is

Figure 2. Nikkei 225 Index Monthly Chart.

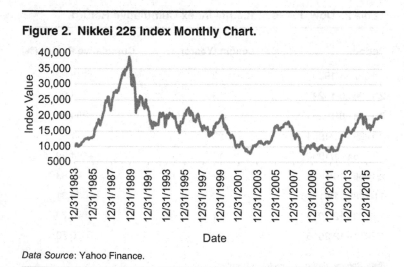

Data Source: Yahoo Finance.

Table 3. Nikkei 225 Index Point-to-Point Cumulative Return Excluding Dividends.

Period	Length (Years)	Cumulative Return (%)
2/1978–12/1989	12.2	+645.14
12/1989–8/2017	27.8	−49.40
6/2007–10/2015	8.4	+10.49
5/2007–8/2017	10.3	+8.56

Data Source: Yahoo Finance and TD Ameritrade.

Figure 3. PowerShares QQQ ETF March 1999–August 2017.

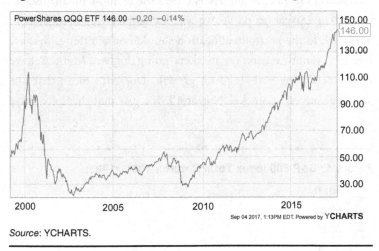

Source: YCHARTS.

reminiscent of the technology boom and bust in the late nineties and early 2000s. If we look at a chart of the PowerShares QQQ ETF, which tracks the technology heavier Nasdaq 100 Index, we can see it took about 15 years from it to eclipse its previous all-time high shown in Figure 3.

If an investor had 15 years until retirement and used the QQQ exchange-traded fund, they would have been left with only the dividends. To be fair, the underlying index did recover its previous high post-2008 market meltdown quicker and began to move higher materially within about 5 years. As we start to understand the concept of the real timeframes investors have around retirement, the concept of protecting and growth becomes important. The value in not taking all of the downside, while still getting some upside will start to make sense. If we shift to the S&P 500 Index, looking at Figure 4, we can see the total returns for the S&P 500 Index from 1966 to 1981.

Compare the previous chart to the famous bull run from 1982 to 1999, which we can visualize in Figure 5.

Stocks historically have offered the best returns. That's why so many investors have equity exposure somewhere in their pie charts. Yet imagine if your assets have little to show for themselves in a 10- or 25-year period. As we will discuss further, a more modern approach to the portfolio allocation should contain things that are not just simply reliant on markets going higher. Markets have experienced long periods of no growth. Does this mean that one shouldn't invest in stocks? Not at all. It's just that there are ways

Figure 4. S&P 500 Index Total Returns 1966–1981.

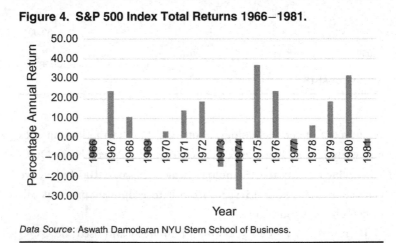

Data Source: Aswath Damodaran NYU Stern School of Business.

Figure 5. S&P 500 Index Total Returns 1992–1999.

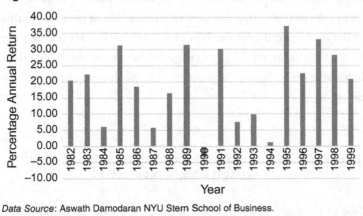

Data Source: Aswath Damodaran NYU Stern School of Business.

to look to capitalize on periods like the 1982–1999 period while still having some hedging protection below the market should you enter periods where sharp corrections or bear markets occur.

One of the interesting things about the two very different periods highlighted above is the interest-rate environments. Think about how rates were rising in the 1970s reaching the peak in 1981. This was the period with a cumulative flat return. Stocks went nowhere and had several negative return years. We will have more to say about this relationship later but suffice to say if you were using the classic discount-to-future earnings by the interest rate, as you brought forward those future earnings at increasing interest rates it surely pushed down stock valuations. Likewise, from the peak in rates over the course of the unbelievable bull run, every time rates went down, future earnings were worth more. I don't think this is a coincidence and something to consider in our current environment of extremely low rates.

The current period, through the end of 2016, has been a tepid run compared to some other historical periods. At the end of 2016, the S&P 500 ETF Symbol: SPY only had a dividend yield of 2.03% (Ycharts, 2016). With low-dividend yields and low-interest rates on fixed income, ex-market movement investor's total returns are coming under pressure. It will be so important to have strategies in the portfolio that can generate risk-adjusted positive returns in flat markets and bear markets as well. Portfolios are a collection of strategies that we look to carry the weight at different times. Increasing one's chances of meeting their goals is so paramount to investing.

1.4. ISSUES WITH TRADITIONAL ASSET ALLOCATIONS IN SHORTER TIME PERIODS

One of the problems with a lot of the classic asset allocation decisions is the fact that they are built using very long-term historical results to produce an average annual return. Then once that average is determined, as a proxy for risk, the standard deviation of annualized investment returns above and below the average. Notice that returns above and below the average are included. While a given year that produces a bad negative return is something most investors would want to avoid, I doubt seriously that when strategies generate way above average returns that many would complain. We will discuss this very issue later, but for now investors have to ask themselves, do I have 70 or 100 years to generate an average that many risk measures are using or do I really only have smaller windows. In smaller windows like a decade or two that many individuals and families have to maximize their retirement saving up to and through retirement may not get the average.

The classical asset allocation which aims to develop a portfolio that offers the highest return with the least amount of volatility, vis-à-vis standard deviation, is including the 17-year period when the Dow Jones Index was up over 1000% and the march down from the 1981 highs in interest rates over a 35-year period. Bonds, as we will explore, are more likely to have much lower returns than the averages. Plus, if interest rates should move materially higher, it could impact stock valuations that could only be replaced with increases to historical growth trends.

1.5. HISTORICAL RETURNS TO DETERMINE PROBABILITIES

Often individuals filling in one of those online retirement calculators wonder what type of return both to assign in the period where they are still working and then post retirement. The next question is what are the chances they can actually achieve those returns? The historical returns are used by many in the investment community to put a probability on what a likely future return is. For example, if we were to utilize historical returns for the S&P 500 Total Return Index and compute what is the percent chance the index would produce a certain return in a given year, we can produce a graph based upon a normal distribution using the average annual historical return and standard deviation. In Figure 6, we can see a concentration of the highest probabilities right around the historical average return.

If you remember the old bell curve, 68% of the values should be contained within 1 standard deviation. In the case of the S&P 500 Total Return, the range of that 1st standard deviation would be between −8.17% and +31.01%. The 2nd standard deviation range, where 95% of the results should be contained within, would be −27.76% to +50.60%. Since the average or mean is 11.42%, there would be exactly a 50% probability the return in a year would be the average itself. One of the criticisms of assigning a normal distribution to market returns is that outliers can happen more frequently. Remember the S&P 500 Index at one point during the Great Recession peak to trough was down around −55%. You probably remember the index notched a 2008 return, including dividends of −36.55%.

If we assign a probability in percentage terms to various negative annual returns, we would see that the chance of some returns that were actually realized by markets would seem rather

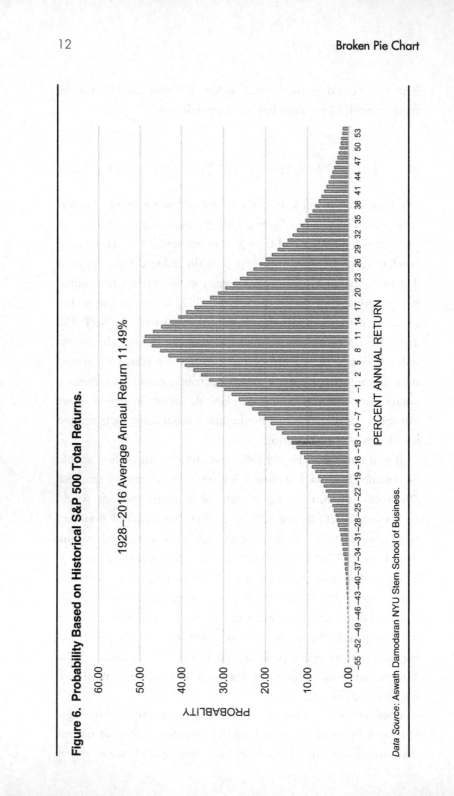

Figure 6. Probability Based on Historical S&P 500 Total Returns.

1928–2016 Average Annaul Return 11.49%

PROBABLITY

PERCENT ANNUAL RETURN

Data Source: Aswath Damodaran NYU Stern School of Business.

Table 4. Annual Negative Return Probabilities Estimated Using Historical S&P 500 Total Returns.

Annual Return Level (%)	Probability (%)
−10	13.71
−15	8.87
−20	5.44
−25	3.15
−30	1.72
−35	0.89
−40	0.42
−45	0.20
−50	0.09

improbable. In Table 4, the percentages represent the probability a return value will be at or below the listed negative return.

The probability percentages represent a return at that level or lower. For example, the probability of a return of −10% or lower (more negative) is 13.71%. It also signifies that there is an 86.29% probability the return in a year will be greater than −10%. As the returns get more negative, the probabilities go down. Thinking about 2008 when the equity market suffered an over −35% down year, the probability through 2016's annual returns only registers a 0.89% that the S&P will return −35% or below. That equates to roughly 110/1 odds. Just because something has a low probability does not mean it can't happen. Consider that from the peak in March of 2007 to the trough in March 2009 the S&P 500 Index was down around 55%. During the last decade, a period from 2000 through 2009, where total returns were a flat 1.16% cumulatively, the markets suffered two of its downside years that today would only have a probability of happening of 0.89% and 3.15%, respectively.

There has been much debate about using a normal distribution probability estimate to market returns. And they are smart to raise those concerns, as the probability percentages may give a false sense of comfort. We know from historical results that while markets "historically" act a certain way over a long time period, the 1987 crash that saw the Dow Jones Index decline −22.6% in a single trading session. The chance of an event like that in a single day would be barely possible in probability terms. The markets on an annual basis have shown the ability to register returns in the tail portion of a normal probability curve. This is a major reason why the options market through pricing various premiums up and down the chain create a volatility expectation that manifests itself in the value one must buy or receive for a particular derivative.

The idea of a low probability or possibility does not mean investors should not consider alternatives to their current pie charts. The National Weather Service posted on their site the odds of being struck by lightning in the United States at 1,083,000 to 1 (NOAA.gov, N.D.). If you convert that to a probability percentage, it would equate to a 0.000092% probability. While a 2008-type year would be less than 1% probability, what if I said you had a 1% chance of being struck by lightning if you went outside your house tomorrow? Would you risk it and go outside? Classical asset allocation in my opinion underestimates the risk for an investor over their most important slices of time in their investment horizon.

While so far our discussion has revolved only around equities, what do the historical returns of the 10-Year Treasury Bond continuous maturity tell us when it comes to the likelihood of achieving a particular annual return going forward? We can see that same probability graph in Figure 7.

Historically, fixed income has experienced less volatility than equities. The 10-Year Treasury Bond experienced an average annual return of 5.18% with a standard deviation of 7.72%. The creates a 1-standard deviation range of −2.54% to +12.90% and a 2-standard deviation range of −10.26% and +20.62%. What if

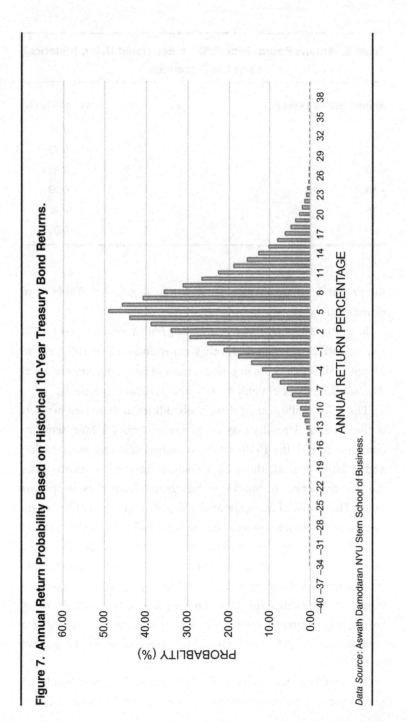

Figure 7. Annual Return Probability Based on Historical 10-Year Treasury Bond Returns.

Data Source: Aswath Damodaran NYU Stern School of Business.

Table 5. Annual Return Probabilities Estimated Using Historical 10-Yr US Treasuries.	
Annual Return Level (%)	Probability (%)
−5	9.36
−7	5.73
−10	2.46
−13	0.93
−15	0.45
−20	0.06

the probabilities are various negative return years? In Table 5 we examine just that.

In 2009, 10-Year Treasuries Bonds had a negative −11.12% return, and as recent as 2013, they experienced a −9.10% return. The probability of those negative returns estimated using historical data would only be roughly 1.80% and 3.30%, respectively.

The point of illustrating these probabilities in these two markets is that historical results may be giving investors a false sense of comfort. Even in the 1970s when coupon yields were much higher and inflation spiked, those high coupon interest payments offset the negative effect on market values from sharp rises in interest rates. The probabilities generated using past results really are no guarantee of future results. The greatest bull run in the markets from November of 1982 to December of 1999 also corresponded with a historical drop in interest rates. Continued reduction in interest rates allowed for equities to gain in price partly because of how future earnings are discounted by a risk-free rate. In other words, when interest rates drop, future earnings — assuming a constant growth rate — provide increased value in the present period.

The challenge with the classic 60/40 portfolio is that bonds are just not going to return much for the foreseeable future. Either rates stay low, which means interest payments will continue to be underwhelming or we see interest rates rise, which will lead to losses in market values. With equities, we are close to the record number of months from a previous recession. At some point, there will most likely be another one.

NEXT STEPS

- Review current allocation.

- Take an inventory of what areas, sectors, regions, asset classes you currently have exposure to and their weighting.

- What type of downside protection is in place if any?

- Gauge how much fear about markets causes your allocation decisions.

- What types of changes did you make in the post 2008–2009 Great Recession period?

- Is your current portfolio designed based upon risk tolerance, age, current assets, or in relation to your current and needed retirement funds?

2

WHY BONDS' PAST PERFORMANCE CAN'T EQUAL FUTURE RESULTS

There is a very real possibility that we are setting up for a lost decade with respect to bonds total returns. To understand the problem, we must examine the reality that investors have enjoyed an unprecedented bull market in bonds that has spanned the better part of 35 years. A market that is moving into a new phase. Bonds traditionally have been used to construct portfolios as a way not only to produce income but to reduce risk compared to equities. Yet in a low to rising interest rate regime what can investors expect? The risk is heightened now for portfolios relying on bonds believing their past performance can continue. As we will outline, there are compelling reasons why it may not be possible in the next decade.

A bond's total return in each year is a combination of the interest received and the change in the underlying market value. They are issued at a face or par value normally equal to $1000. The rate of interest paid annually is the coupon. If a bond has a par value of $1000 and pays $40 annually, we would say the bond has a 4% coupon. An investor who buys a bond is essentially making a loan to a company, government, or municipality for a set term. If purchased at par, they would pay $1000 and receive annual interest payments. Then at the end of the term, they would look to get their principle back at par value, as the bond matures.

They can also be purchased on the open market where the market value can be above or below par value. In this instance, we commonly would reference the yield to maturity, which gives an annualized rate of return accounting for both the interest received and any gain or loss to par value. For example, if a bond was purchased on the open market for $900 and matures at $1000 par value, the gain one would receive in principle would be annualized for the remaining time to maturity. Likewise, a bond purchased greater than par value at a premium would account for the loss in principle when calculating its yield to maturity.

While examining an individual bond helps to provide clarity, most investors don't purchase them individually. Instead they use mutual funds or exchange-traded funds. Funds represent a collection of assets that wind up having a blended effective duration. Duration is important, as the longer the duration, the greater the market value sensitivity to changes in interest rates. Bond market values typically have an inverse relationship to interest rates. When rates go up, bond values move lower and vice versa. The longer the duration, the more cash flows will be affected and cause an adjustment to the market price. How much do changes in interest rates cause market values to change?

Regarding interest rate changes, they are normally referred to in basis points, or bips (BPS) for short. A change of 1% would be a 100-basis point change. A half-percent change would be a 50-basis point difference. In Table 6 we see what a change in rates can do depending on how much time left until maturity. We will assume a current interest rate of 2.5% and the current price of $1000 or par for illustrations sake, and payments would be paid semiannually.

Remember we started this chapter referencing a powerful bull market for bonds? In September of 1981, the U.S. Treasury 10-Year Bond had a coupon yield of 15.84%. Since posting that high, we have seen yields continue to fall. You probably are starting to realize that falling yields have been aiding market returns

Table 6. Changes to Bond Market Value When Rates Move Higher or Lower 100–200 BPS.

New Rate (%)	2-Year Maturity (%)	5-Year Maturity (%)	10-Year Maturity (%)	20-Year Maturity (%)	30-Year Maturity (%)
0.5	+4.0	+9.9	+19.5	+38.0	+55.7
1.5	+2.0	+4.8	+ 9.3	+11.7	+24.1
2.5 (current)					
3.5	−1.9	−4.6	−8.4	−14.3	−18.5
4.5	−3.8	−8.9	−16.0	−26.2	−32.7

for all those bond mutual funds for the last 35 years. Not only have bond funds benefited from increasing market values, the interest payments while falling have been historically much higher than today. Think about it, interest rates go down, bond prices move up. All with higher coupon payments so almost a double benefit. Of course post 2008, interest rates have remained low, so the total return is more dependent on changes to market values. In Figure 8 we can see the historical yield of the 10-year treasury bond.

It would be difficult to imagine a scenario where rates would go so far negative that it would help bonds achieve the same type of returns purely in market value over the next 10–20 years. As of this writing, the United States has not seen its treasuries posting negative yields such as those witnessed in Germany, Japan, and Switzerland. Plus, as we will discuss, we have a coupon problem that not only will make total returns more difficult, but we lose the ability to cover up losses due to rising rates. Can you imagine today having the opportunity to buy a 10- or 30-year treasury

Figure 8. Monthly Historical 10-Year Treasury Bond Yields 1962–2016.

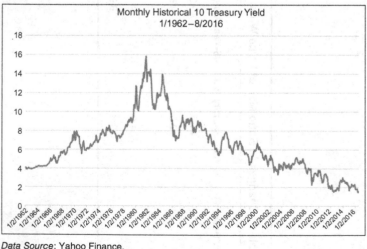

Data Source: Yahoo Finance.

bond paying 15% annually in interest? As we look back, one must wonder whether this was an anomaly. The Bank of England has historical interest rates back through 1694. The period from the mid-1970s through 1981 saw the highest rates in any period starting from 1694 forward to today (Bank of England, 2016). In Figure 9 we can view the historical landscape of rates in England.

This collection of rates represents a combination of the bank rate, minimum lending rate, minimum band 1 dealing rate, repo rate, and official bank rate (Bank of England, 2016). The point of taking a long view at rates at the Bank of England is to highlight the anomaly of the spike in the last century. In the longer run, rates have been more stable. Although with rates at historically low levels, this creates interest rate risk for investors should rates revert to the mean. The run up in rates to what would seem like untenable levels historically points to a historic spike. The 35+ years where falling rates caused bonds to rise from those atmospheric levels.

Figure 9. Bank of England Changes in Bank Rate 1694–2016.

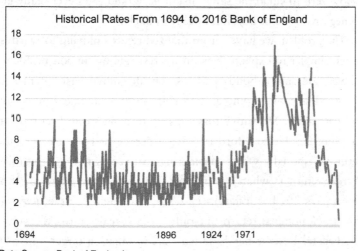

Data Source: Bank of England.

Now the Federal Reserve at the end of 2015 raised rates for the
first time since cutting to nearly zero during the Great Recession.
Some are afraid of a period of heightened inflation and rising rates.
Primarily, because of the amount of public debt we have not only
in the United States but around the world. We've already shown
what can happen to bond values especially at the longer end of the
curve. If you suspend the belief that interest rates can go far below
the zero bound, there is little left to potentially gain by falling
rates. Should rising rates materialize, it puts bond investors in a
tough spot. Keep durations short wherein a normal yield curve
rates remain lower or try to reach toward the far end of the curve.
Yet that extra margin of interest probably isn't worth the extra
risk. Further problematic is in traditional asset allocations; longer
duration treasuries were preferred as they provided a better historical hedge. In traditional recessions, as equities sold off, investors
flocked to the safe haven of bonds. Plus, what does the Fed typically do during recession? You guessed it: they lower rates to try
to stimulate the economy thus aiding bond returns. The last recession started with a Fed Funds rate of 4.5%. To get to zero that
was 450 basis points of cutting. Can they really get rates that far
below zero to equal the same distance? Would rates ever really go
to negative 10% or beyond. Highly unlikely.

The problem we have for annualized returns moving forward is
much simpler to explain. It is an interest rate or coupon problem.
Lower rates mean bonds pay less on an annual basis. It means
there is less capital coming in to help offset or augment moves in
market values. Most investors looking to build toward retirement
may not be able to afford to have a decade or two of low bond
returns. Especially when considering real versus nominal returns.
A real return is what is left after considering for inflation. If a
bond pays 3% but inflation is 2.5%, we would say the investor
has a 3% nominal return but only a 0.5% real return. We know
the Federal Reserve has broadcast a 2% inflation target, but real
returns across the world have been under pressure.

As we mentioned in the first chapter, historically continuous maturing 10-Year T-bonds have returned from 1928 to 2016 (Damodarin, 2016), an average annual total return of 5.18%. A total return includes both changes up or down in the underlying market value as well as interest received. You might, especially in this current low-rate environment, think not bad, right? The challenge is included in those returns were higher annual interest payments collected. Plus, when rates went down during a year that also aided a positive market value return. Consider Figure 10, which illustrates the annual total return with and without the coupon payments included.

What we realize is that looking at historical returns over a long period, if we only used the average annual change up or down in the market value of 10-year T-Bonds, it would only average an annual gain of 0.22%. Now some might take issue with removing interest payments and only isolating the returns attributed to the market value as the total return is a combination of the coupon payments received and any underlying change. They would not be wrong to point that out. Yet the reason to highlight the difference is simply to point out that over a long period of time, more of a

Figure 10. Average Annual 10-Year T-Bond Total Return versus Market Returns Only.

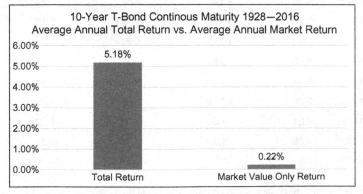

Data Source: Aswath Damodaran NYU Stern School of Business.

bonds annual return is due to the interest it pays out. Further during the periods included, coupon rates were higher. In some cases, much higher. So, if we think about a decade of extended historically lower rates can we really expect bonds to produce the same types of returns on an annual basis as they have in the past? If interest rates stay low and flat going forward, we shouldn't expect more than a lower annual return because interest rates are low.

The other scenario gets a bit trickier. This would be if we start to see an extended period of rising rates. Investors holding bond funds would see their market values stressed, especially if rates rise at a rapid pace and to higher levels than currently forecast. Higher coupon payments in each year helped to muffle losses in market value. Consider Table 7, which illustrates the period between 1970 and 1980 that saw rates move from 6.9% to 12.84% in the 10-Year Treasury Bond.

Table 7. 1970–1980 10-Year T-Bond Returns.

Year	Coupon Rate (%)	Change in Rate from Previous Year (%)	Total Return (%)	Market Value Only Change (%)
1970	6.39	−1.26	16.75	10.36
1971	5.93	−0.46	9.79	3.86
1972	6.36	+0.46	2.82	−3.54
1973	6.74	+0.38	3.66	−3.08
1974	7.43	+0.69	1.99	−5.44
1975	8.00	+0.57	3.61	−4.39
1976	6.87	−1.13	15.98	9.11
1977	7.69	+0.82	1.29	−6.40
1978	9.01	+1.32	−0.78	−9.79
1979	10.39	+1.38	0.67	−9.72
1980	12.84	+2.45	−2.99	−15.83

Data Source: Aswath Damodaran NYU Stern School of Business.

A few things to note here. First one can see the return due to changes in market value had several negative years. Second, because interest rates were so high it produced a positive total return. For example, in 1980, the yield increased by 2.45% points to 12.84%. That high coupon payment reduced a market value only return of −15.83% to only −2.99%. Now imagine today if rates went from 2.5% to 5.0%? The market value loss would be similar but instead of having a robust 12.84% to help defer the loss, we would only enjoy 2.5% in coupon payments thus still leaving a remaining material loss for the year. We can see in Figure 11 that without the added return derived from the interest, bonds market derived returns are a bit less appealing.

By subtracting the total annual return by the annual coupon payment, we can see that the 10-Year Treasury had quite a number of negative "market return" years. Again, the reason to bring this up is the fact that the lower the coupon, the lower contribution to the total return. Yes, when rates rose in the 1970s, bonds had years with positive returns. However, many of those years had substantially greater coupon percentage yields than today. We are

Figure 11. Annual Return 10-Year Treasury Bond Market Only Return Ex-Coupon %.

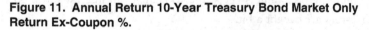

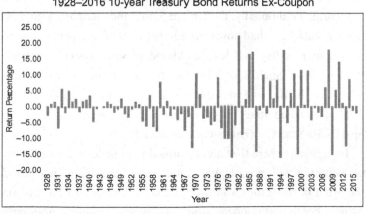

Data Source: Aswath Damodaran NYU Stern School of Business.

in a low interest rate environment so any material increases in yields may result in bond losses not experienced before.

The reason to outline where returns came from is to understand that increases in market interest rates would hurt more when rates are low. The coupon interest payments can't help total returns every year. Since we've determined that much of historical returns are more heavily based on the interest paid, when rates are low, our expected total return should remain low as well. Bond, yields since the height of rates in 1981, have been falling, and during the period between 1981 and 2016, the average annual total return was 8.46% versus the 1928–2016 period where it was 5.81%. During the 1970–1980 period, the total return was just 4.8% — when guess what? That's right; the average coupon annual payment was 7.9%. Once again, we see that higher coupon interest helped to cover up and exceed market losses.

As we look to the decade ahead, if rates remain low, investors may simply look to expect an average annual total return right around where the coupon rate is. Unfortunately, if we get a period of rising interest rates, investors will feel the brunt of those moves much more, since smaller annual interest payments won't be able to mute market value swings due to changes in interest rates. So, investors are caught a bit.

One of the things that we continue to see is lower rates around the world. Traditionally, the United States and Germany's government bonds have had lower yields because of the perception of having more safety and less likelihood of some systemic default. Back in 2012, Spain's 10-Year Government Bond yield was over 6% while the United States that same year was under 2%. In mid-2017, the United States' 10-Year yield was just worth of 2% while Spain's 10-Year Government sits around 1.50%.

If rates stay where they are, returns should be lower. If rates rise, coupon rates will move higher, yet existing bond holdings will feel the brunt of those moves in their market values. As we touched on earlier, bonds with longer durations would be most negatively impacted thus suffering the most decline in market values.

In 2013, bonds had a negative return year. If we use the IShares 20 + Year Treasury Bond ETF and the IShares 7- to 10-Year Treasury Bond ETF, we can get an indication of how bond yields rising during that period affected performance as in Figure 12.

The longer duration as expected sold off more with a negative −14.8% return versus the negative −7.24% number. 2013 was the summer of the so-called "Taper Tantrum" after the United States Federal Reserve Bank let it be known that they may slow the pace of asset purchases as part of their quantitative easing program. To put into perspective though, rates on both the 10-Year Treasury Bond and 20-Year Treasury Bond moved higher as we can see in Figure 13.

From the beginning of 2013 to year end, the interest rate on the 10-Year Treasury jumped over 63% while the rate on the 20-Year Treasury moved higher by over 41%. Think about what would happen if rates actually do rise over the next decade. Especially, since they won't be paying hefty premiums like in the late 1970s.

Figure 12. 2013 Annual Percent Change IShares 20 + and 7- to 10-Year Treasury Bond ETFs.

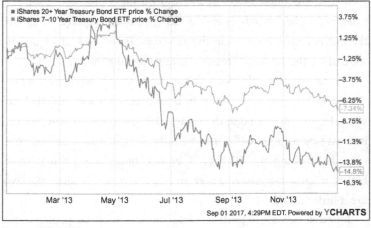

Source: YCHARTS.

Figure 13. 2013 10-Year and 20-Year Treasuries Bond Yields.

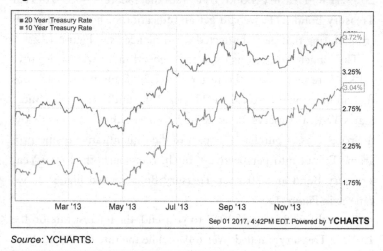

Source: YCHARTS.

2.1. INFLATION IMPACT ON BOND YIELDS

This would make sense since people normally demand a rate of return that exceeds the rate of inflation. This would make sense since interest rates are part of what people demand for investments. Inflation impacts the risk-free rate used in analysis of performance, discounted cash flows, and business projects. If interest rates are higher, bonds being issued would be required to satisfy the current rate of return in the markets. If we look at Figure 14 we can see the 10-Year Treasury rate versus the inflation rate.

We can see generally bond yields move to a good degree in tandem with inflation. Sometimes inflation settled above the 10-Year yield. From 1981 through the early 2000s, the spread between the interest rate paid annually and the inflation rate had a nice positive spread. Meaning the 10-Year Treasury bond was paying out a higher interest rate above where inflation stood. Recently, the two are a little closer.

Inflation is very important when we think about planning for retirement or retirees themselves. One's nominal return is simply

Figure 14. Historical U.S. Inflation Rate versus 10-Year Treasury Rate.

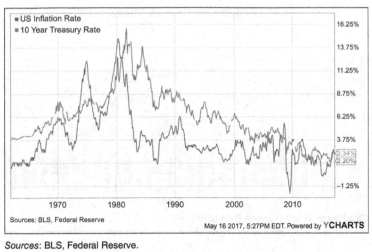

Sources: BLS, Federal Reserve.

Sources: BLS, Federal Reserve.

what they might return on a percentage basis in a year. Their real rate of return is their nominal return — inflation rate. If a portfolio makes 3%, but inflation is 3.5%, we would say the investor realized a negative real return of 0.5%. Retirees will plan to withdraw a certain percentage annually. If their rate of real return can't exceed inflation by much, there could be issues. Consider Figure 15, which illustrates the difference between the PCE (Personal Consumption Expenditures), excluding food and energy, quarterly annualized increase or decrease along with the 10-Year Treasury Quarterly Rate.

The difference between the two is a good indication of the real interest rates, which represent the rate post adjusting for inflation. The graph left axis runs from −4% to +10%. You can see that in the 1970s, the real interest rate dipped below 0% as inflation spiked higher than the 10-Year Treasury nominal rate. As rates crested in 1981, the spread between treasury yields and inflation widened, which indicates the investor enjoyed a higher real interest rate. As rates have continued lower from the early 1980's highs,

Figure 15. 10-Year Treasury Constant Maturity Historical Quarterly Minus PCE Index.

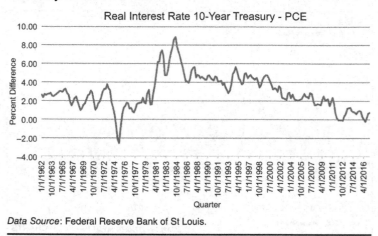

Data Source: Federal Reserve Bank of St Louis.

the spread has continued to narrow. Recently as 2012 and 2016, the spread went negative indicating a yield that did not outdo inflation. By the way, if we had the benefit of knowing what we know now back in say 1981, this book would be one page and be titled *Buy 30-Year Treasury Bonds and Check Back in 30 Years*. As inflation moved lower, the fixed coupon payments would have been generating real returns better than equities. Of course that's revisionist history and Monday morning quarterbacking at its worst. The point is that rates and inflation have converged. If rates stay low, why would we expect real rates of return to increase over inflation?

Without getting too in depth, the ability for assets to last is a combination of the withdrawal rate, annual rate of return, and inflation. If expenses in each year are $40,000 and inflation is at 3%, then you would need $41,236 after adjusting for annual inflation the next year. We will talk about the importance of the sequence of returns as it relates to both the period before and after retirement later. For now, hopefully you can start to understand the idea of producing real returns that can support your income needs in retirement.

With a modern pie chart, the holding cost of bonds and income might be shifted to alternative strategies. Part of the reason for increasing the percentage of a portfolio into bonds is to create a less risky portfolio. One with less volatility. What we will find out though is that perhaps the ability to hold equities with a more limited downside may do the de-risking for us.

Another aspect on bonds that should be brought up is how much utility do they really offer aside from a hope to keep up with inflation and a slice in the portfolio that will hold up in market downturns? If we think about the average annual return on 10-Year Treasury Bonds being just worth of 5% and the average risk-free rate of about 3.5%, they have only produced a real annual a little above the risk-free rate. The period from 1981, which saw the apex in rates, to 2016 just before the short end of the curve began to rise off its zero floor, it provided bonds with a boost to annual returns. Later we will delve into some common ways to measure a risk-adjusted return. Moving forward, with the current interest rate environment, it may be some time before the fixed income asset class provide any real effect to many popular ratios besides reducing historical volatility. Of course if interest rates should spike, that may come under severe pressure as well.

Fixed income also has some additional challenges ahead. You may be familiar with the Federal Reserve and how they maintained a zero-interest rate policy nicknamed ZIRP. Some central banks around the world even instituted negative interest rate policies, NIRP for short. On top of that, the Federal Reserve's balance sheet exploded to over $4 Trillion dollars when they instituted several rounds of quantitative easing, which included buying U.S. government treasury bonds and mortgage-backed bonds.

The Fed has signaled their intent to wind down their balance sheet by either not reinvesting funds from maturing issues or actually strategically selling bonds at various points in the yield curve. We will explore this topic further, but safe to say many people are interested to see how this will work as it has never been tried

before. Will the Fed invert the yield curve or cause selling pressure
that sees a liquidity crunch to the space?

We know that the way of doing things is ingrained for many
people. The idea that a combination of stocks and bonds allocated
appropriate to one's age and risk toleration produces an ideal
portfolio. Over the long term, it would be tough to break down
that belief. Yet as we've been alluding to investors' need to
approach one- or two-decade periods as stages. Ones that require
an approach that will fall short, should the historical averages not
be realized.

As we will see next, funds designed to be a set-it-and-forget-it
solution, rightly or wrongly, were misunderstood as to the true
risk in 2008.

NEXT STEPS

- What is your current portfolio weighting toward bonds?

- Of current bond allocation, how are holdings weighting by
  type?

- What is the effective duration of the portfolio?

- What is the current expected annual yield?

- Should interest rates stay low, how would that affect your
  asset growth?

- How would inflation affect your estimated retirement income
  requirements?

- How would a spike in interest rates affect the value of the
  bond portion of your portfolio?

3

TARGET DATE SURPRISE

In the early 1990s, Target Date Funds were introduced, but by 2009, the Securities and Exchange Commission was holding hearings (SEC.GOV, 2010) in the aftermath of 2008. In the depths of the financial crisis, I can remember individual investors coming up to me with statements asking how their accounts could be down so much so close to retirement. I remember some saying they were bad products while others pointed to lack of understanding of what they really were. While the exact make-up of the funds' portfolios differed from one to another, by and large they created a pie chart that aligned with what classical asset allocation says is the right mix. They didn't say they would hedge downside risk.

3.1. 2008 GREAT RECESSION AND NEAR-TERM TARGET DATE FUNDS

When 2008 happened, investors in 2010 target date funds saw drawdowns of up to 40% or more at the trough of the market. That understandably could be quite upsetting given how close in proximity retirement was. But the target date funds by and large did what they were designed to do: automatically adjust between various asset classes. If we believe that traditional pie charts may be outdated for the next 20 years, then a fund relying on those ideals may disappoint. If interest rates should spike, the next challenges for some funds would be bond market values declining significantly. So, what are Target Date Funds and what is the rationale behind them?

The intention to create a set it and forget it funds that individual investors could choose and not think about was well intentioned. If you are of the belief that one should contain the classic age-based allocation, and that allocation should be shifted when age milestones are reached, then target date funds mostly do just that. Instead of someone working at a company and needing to remember to choose less equity funds and more bond funds the older they got in their 401k, the target date fund itself would internally do the shifting automatically. They wouldn't have to worry about rebalancing or needing to study various retirement plan choices or fund families. Do it once, and the fund will take care of the rest.

This seemed to solve the problem of an investor's portfolio remaining age-appropriate based on where they were in their working lives. If, in 1995, one believed they would retire in 2010, choose the 2010 Target Date Fund. Not only would the fund internally automatically tilt more toward bonds closer to retirement, it would continue post-retirement and continue to adjust down equity exposure to not only fixed income but also short duration instruments and cash like vehicles. A thirty-year-old in the workplace today might choose a 2045 or 2050 target date fund.

Setting aside some variations in performance of the same dated funds, they operated as they said they would. Simply, someone far away from retirement would have almost all their assets in equities. Despite the financial crisis surprises, as of 2014 (Bary, 2014), more than 20% of all retirement assets or $2 Trillion was held in various target date funds. Remember the size of the market when we discuss some of the risks as to the exposure that is currently in the marketplace for retirees.

3.2. TARGET FUND COMPOSITION

The way target date funds work is at various trigger points allocation targets shift. They refer to it as a glide path. Think about a
plane coming in for a landing. Typically, they begin their descent
and follow an orderly path toward the runway slowly declining in
altitude. They touch down and then taxi across the runway to the
gate. Passengers deplane and shift to another type of transporta-
tion for the rest of their journey. An investor saving for retirement
is in a similar flight plan that sees the high altitude of equities
move from almost all their portfolio down to only a less significant
piece post-retirement. From Figure 16 we can see a sample glide
path starting at 25 years to retirement, retirement at zero years,
and out forward 25 years into retirement.

In our graphic, you notice how younger investors' portfolios
target more equities and adjustments at each stage. With 5 years to
retirement, we see a 64/30/6% allocation across stocks, fixed
income, and short-term fixed income. At retirement, equities dip to
55% finally being reduced to 20% in year 25 post-retirement.
Remember these are classic portfolio pie charts that shift depending on someone's investing stages. What that means is that

**Figure 16. Sample Allocation Path 25 Years Before and After
Retirement.**

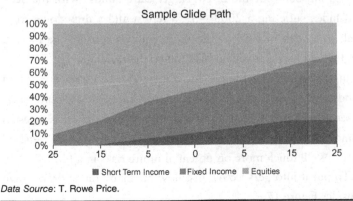

Data Source: T. Rowe Price.

someone 5 years out in un-hedged equity has almost 65% of the portfolio open to catastrophic downside risk. In today's environment, the 6% piece is earning next to nothing in short-term income while 30% in bonds has historically low yields while possessing interest rate and inflation risk.

3.3. HEARINGS POINT TO ISSUES WITH TARGET DATE FUNDS

According to a fact sheet on issues and proposals (SEC.Gov, 2010) outlined by the Securities and Exchange Commission, target date funds suffered from a few deficiencies. The first one they alluded to the "2008 experience" where investors in 2010-dated funds averaged 24% in losses at year end in 2008. They also pointed out that due to how different one fund to another created their allocations results ranged between −9% loss to negative −41% at year end 2008 (SEC.gov, 2010). Now the market didn't reach bottom until March of 2009. During that time, many 2010-dated funds saw max drawdowns almost equal to equity only losses.

In a report by the U.S. Senate's Committee on Aging (GPO.gov, 2009), they pointed to how different the equity allocation percentage was from fund to fund citing a range of 24% to 68% in equities during 2008 for the 2010 Target Date Funds. With the S&P 500 Index suffering a 2008 −37% return and a drawdown from peak to trough of −56%, the more equity exposure the more a fund would be negatively impact due to their decline.

In the future, if a fund is heavily weighted in longer duration bonds and there was a spike in interest rates, that would cause losses as well. Some bond funds during the financial crisis invested in mortgage-backed securities or credit-default swaps saw outsized losses. We'll touch more on potential future risks in a bit.

To put it into perspective just how far many funds drew down consider Figure 17.

Figure 17. Select 2010 Target Date Fund's October 2007 Peak to March 2009 Trough.

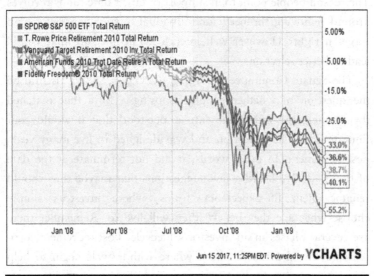

One of the reasons for the differences in performance was the way managers dealt with how to make sure assets lasted through the drawdown period. There are varying ideas on what the right asset allocation mix might be. Managers using the same methods of asset allocation adjust the levers in the pie chart. I wouldn't be surprised if in the next decade there aren't complaints about bond fund performance within target date funds, should we get a real spike in interest rates.

The SEC 2010 write-up suggested as one of the remedies that funds should make more disclosures about their exact asset allocation. There should be more charts and graphs showing those funds glide paths. An investor knowing what is in their fund is always a good idea. Of course they should have that information. Yet, would putting pressure on the individual to decide their percentage allocation to various asset classes eliminate the very reason target date funds were created? Wouldn't that mean that investors would then have to decide between target date funds? Or perhaps create a different allocation, piecing together other funds? The reason people point to in support of target date funds revolves around removing the need for individual rebalancing. Set it and forget it right? However well intended, I'm not sure that would lead to better selection.

The Senate Committee on Aging (GPO.gov, 2009) also raised the question of whether people choosing a fund that matched their anticipated retirement date understood that it would continue to adjust its allocation and was designed to live many years post-retirement. In other words, it did not terminate at the date of the fund. I've heard a few suggestions that maybe they should rename them life-expectancy funds, where investors simply choose what age they believe they will live to. Remember there are several phases in an investor's lifecycle. Post-retirement, people enter the drawdown phase where withdrawals begin to help cover expenses. Assets are meant to be treated differently through those cycles.

Target Date Retirement Funds are the opposite of, say, a college education saving account. College saving funds have a terminal event in mind. Your kid goes to college and needs to start paying tuition. Knowing that the money presumably is going to be withdrawn over the next 4 years (we hope), the risk is ratcheted way down to reduce the volatility and exposure to equity risk. Consider Table 8, which highlights a sample 529 College Saving Plan allocation for a student 19 + years of age.

In the case of college-funding accounts, the event is terminal and most likely will all be withdrawn over a couple years. Therefore, it has almost no equity exposure at the beginning of the withdrawal period. Retirement accounts should operate differently in that monies need to stretch and last over many years to provide supplemental income. A college-funding account in theory should last 4 years for most.

Now the Committee on Aging also included in their report language that seemed to infer that many retirees take a lump-sum

Table 8. Nebraska State Nest 529 Age-Based Index Allocation 19 Years and Older.

Domestic equity	4%
International equity	1%
International bond	2%
Fixed income	38%
Cash equivalents	55%

Data Source: NEST 529 College Savings.

withdrawal from their 401k's at retirement. The danger they alluded to was that if an investor intends to target a one-time withdrawal at retirement for expenses, having any equity exposure like many target date funds contain in the year of retirement increases risk of the funds not being available to withdraw. It would seem to deduce that a retiree planning for a one-time withdrawal might have a portfolio designed closer to one of a student in their first year of college. Should those individuals have chosen a lump-sum withdrawal 2010 fund? Regardless there would not be a guarantee against loss.

The idea of the target date fund was well intentioned. Many of the funds set up portfolios that looked to change the blend of portfolios as one marched through various time lines in their working and retired phases. While there is some debate about what the right percentage mix should be, by and large funds executed on the idea that they would make changes internally so investors would not have to. The proposals (SEC, 2010) to disclose more are well intentioned as well. People choosing target date funds should know what is in the fund and how it will change. They should know they can lose money pre- and post-retirement target date. They also should know that it really is only constructed using age to determine portfolio weighting.

3.4. TARGET DATE FUNDS DO NOT INDIVIDUALIZE ADVICE

The problem with these one-size-fits-all approaches is that while convenient and easy, they don't fully address each person's individual situation. One of the questions I get a lot is, do I have enough to retire at such and such age? Am I where I need to be at this age? Real guidance is much more personal. Using a proposed retirement age to determine one's allocation doesn't address what a person's real needs are. Someone retiring at 50 versus 70 would have different requirements for income from a longevity standpoint. What if they also have a pension from another employer? What if their spouse has assets?

The real answer to the question "do I have enough?" is much more specific to the individual. Sometimes it's made to seem more complex than it really is. Yet, if you look at specific situations, the investing approach can vary. Most programs that try to figure out whether someone will have enough to cover expenses in retirement combine several inputs and assumptions to show whether funds will last. Sure, age is part of it. But age alone is less than adequate to determine what someone's needs really are.

Age only matters in so much as there is a life expectancy that theoretically determines how long your money needs to last. A married couple would have a combined outlook. You take assumptions about future inflation, annual cumulative returns, future expenses and produce a theoretical answer about the types of returns needed to meet a retirement income goal.

Target date funds do nothing to address the individual situations. Take someone who is nearing retirement and has plenty of assets to last them through the drawdown period. They ran the numbers and figures based upon their future income needs they could get by with a nominal return simply to keep pace with inflation. This investor within a year or two till retirement might have more than half their accounts in un-hedged equities. Would they really want to open themselves up to taking a 2008-style hit when they could take their foot off the pedal?

Of course, many say that most retirees have not saved enough to last or provide income that they seek. For them do they need to be more aggressive under the theory that they may run out of money anyway? Having a good portion or the majority in bonds yielding so little, with so much interest rate risk might not be appropriate. Many investors really need more equity exposure than a target date might call for. Simply a person being at a certain age may not fully address their requirement to find more growth to compensate for underfunded accounts. Later we will explore how a good-hedged equity strategy that minimizes the downside but get most of the upside would be far safer than having straight stock funds. But again, the target date fund plies the same approach to everyone in that age range.

Some might argue that a worker participating in a 401k plan could address their specific circumstances by switching to a different target date. This would allow them to tweak the underlying portfolio so that the assets would be allocated differently. Once again that puts the responsibility on the saver. It asks them to get into portfolio design and planning. Remember the set it and forget it goal of target date funds?

These products also don't consider the owner's outside assets and how that might affect the portfolios design. When I sit down with people, the process is much more personal. Looking at all the assets across the spectrum. What might social security potentially yield? Are there pensions from previous employers? The outside asset deal is important. In a vacuum, a target date fund and the manager believing it's the optimal portfolio arrangement would have the fund set up to be perfectly aligned. Rebalancing would happen to bring things back into alignment. Thinking about how often people move jobs, it would be more improbable that investors have a single portfolio.

People have old 401k's, IRAs, and individual accounts spread around. Married couples multiply this issue by doubling possible collection of assets. For target date funds that simply assign an allocation based on one's age does nothing to address how these various assets fit in with what the fund is doing. Choosing a portfolio based only on a single component "age" takes none of that into account. Doesn't calculate whether the assets are sufficient or not for where the investor is in their lifecycle.

In 2008, the origination for the public debate on target date funds, people had a chance to think about whether they were still the best option for many investors. Yet assets have continued to pour into them. Some predict (Steyer, 2014) that by 2019 target date funds will reach $2 Trillion in assets. Much of that growth is due to workers being defaulted into whatever mutual fund company's product is available in their 401k plan. Others choose a fund based on their expected retirement date in self-directed accounts. With that much money moving into these vehicles, you wonder whether the pain will increase should we have another serious market correction. We've seen what can happen to equity allocations in the 2008 drawdown. The next problem may be a market correction in equities. It may also be a spike in interest rates, which would punish bond mutual funds. Those same committees that debated whether there was too high a percentage in equities for funds close to retirement target will be singing a different song. If rates spike, hearings might focus on why funds held so much in bonds when the expectation was a rise in rates? Hindsight is always 20/20. But do investors really have more of an understanding of these funds today than they had 10 years ago?

We know that not all these fund families use the same percentage allocation for their like-dated funds. But what investors may not know is how sensitive their bond portion is to interest rates. What is the effective duration of that slice of the pie chart? With yields so low will they try and reach for yield in lower rated issues? Some invest a portion in international equities and bonds. This brings in some currency risk. I've heard that others may start to add commodities or real estate (REITS). Some of the risks may not be readily evident to the non-discerning eye.

While many of the target date mutual funds insulated 2008 equity losses with their bond holdings, one of the worst performing funds saw its fixed income portion suffer steep losses. A good number of these funds invest in a group of their own family's other mutual funds. So, let's say an investor buys Company A's Target Date 2020 fund. That fund may then invest in Company A's core bond fund, large cap equity fund, international fund, and so on. In 2008, one firm's 2010 target date fund invested in assets like mortgage-backed securities via one of the bond funds held in the portfolio (Hale, 2017). This lead to losses more like a 100% equity holding would've had.

As I said earlier, the firms offering these funds by and large are doing what they intend to, which is creating portfolios that start at one point and get more conservative as the holder ages. They are using the classic asset allocation by choosing to diversify more often than not between some mix of stocks and some mix of bonds. If you believe that investors should just keep using classic portfolio design, then the debate is really what the percentage should be at a given age. I do believe the intention is grounded in the belief that left onto themselves, most investors would make choices that might be less optimal. Some might be too conservative and others might try and time markets only to miss out as they ride out periods in cash.

The important point though is target date funds however well intentioned don't individualize the process. They don't offer true hedges against market declines when investors need it most. If the construction is based on years and years of historical averages and we enter periods of no growth or continued low-interest rates they may not produce returns needed. If rates spike in the years before the retirement date, there could be considerable losses in the fixed income portions.

The truth is many people building toward retirement may need more growth than they think. This means they need equity like investments. The better approach would be to use hedged equity strategies. This allows for equity allocation but with a safety net. Volatility as we will get into, has become an emerging asset class and should have a place in the portfolio. Remember the three phases: accumulation, base growth, and distribution. Having strategies that can strive to optimize investment returns and risk should be paramount. And they must be customized for the individual's own needs.

One of the main debates around target date funds is just how much each asset class should have and at what age. One side says the equity portion was overweighted and that extra percent allocation caused increased losses. That crowd would suppose more assets should be in "safer" fixed income assets. Others would say investors still need equity exposure for the very reason of the extra growth required even closer toward retirement. They worry about "longevity" risk, which implies there is a real risk that someone will outlast their assets. This very debate first points to the problem of generalizing an allocation based solely on one's age. Instead, what if the individual's portfolio already had enough to last well into retirement. That extra equity percentage is putting that retirement at risk. Someone else being too conservative when they are under capitalized might be no better off thus outliving their assets anyway.

If we get back to the reason why fixed income traditionally has been included in portfolios, it was to reduce volatility, reduce risk, and try to generate the best risk-adjusted overall return. In updated pie charts, it would seem if more growth is still sought and prioritized then why not invest using more hedged equity strategies that do reduce the downside, something bonds are utilized for, but give investors more of a chance for outsized upside returns?

While target date funds objectives are simply to shift asset allocations around based on age, the moves in 2008 had real consequences. Consider how much of difference large losses so close to retirement would actually mean. If we use some hypothetical assumptions and then plot in a large 30% drawdown graphically it can illustrate the impact. We will assume someone has 2 full working years left until they retire. At age 64, retiring at 66, they have a balance of $615,118. Their current salary is $114,947 and expect only a 1% increase each remaining year. Of that salary they are putting away 15% toward their retirement savings. We have plotted in an inflation expectation of 2.5% a year. Post-retirement they will receive approximately $18,000 annually in social security, which is not increased for any cost of living adjustments, or COLA. Finally, they require 65% of their final years' salary as income year one of retirement, which of course will increase in raw amount each year for inflation.

The difference in our two hypothetical scenarios is that within our first graph, the investor enjoys a smooth average annual return of 7% pre-retirement and 6% post-retirement. Figure 18 illustrates what their equity curve might look like.

Now we look at the same underlying assumptions but instead change just one thing. For the investor in their age 64 year, instead of earning 7% with all other assumptions being the same, they instead suffer a 30% loss in that year (Figure 19).

The difference is that one bad year caused their assets to run out at age 76 instead of age 82. That one year created a 6-year difference in how long their money lasted in retirement, leaving them only to live on social security. Of course this only uses assumptions

Figure 18. Hypothetical Equity Curve Using Assumptions with No Large Drawdown.

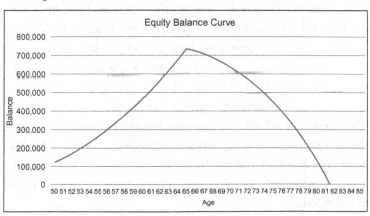

Figure 19. Hypothetical Equity Curve Using Assumptions with Large Drawdown.

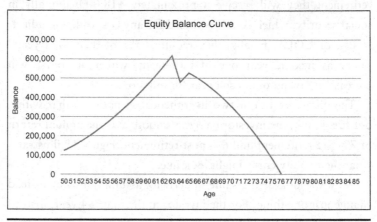

and does not include equity in a house or other asset. The illustration does show that without a real hedge or downside protection that is more fixed, once again asset allocation can only provide so much protection against bad markets.

Target date funds unfortunately continue to be misunderstood as many investors continue to put money in them. 401k funds use them as a default option more and more as workers sign up. As we saw in our discussion on why diversification fails, more and more, a greater concentration of assets are being funneled into broad market exchange-traded funds, which could increase drawdowns during market selloffs. These age-based allocation vehicles do little to understand those that they are trying to help. In some cases, they may underestimate the growth needs of pre-retirees and other times not adjust once someone has met their planning goals. While 401ks unfortunately have more limited choices, individual retirement accounts and taxable accounts now offer the ability to access strategies which look to balance both growth and risk management.

NEXT STEPS

- Review brokerage statements to determine current allocation in target date funds.

- Research the age-based glide path allocation for the family of target date funds.

- Review performance during market selloffs.

- Get a financial plan to determine what future investment return needs may be.

- Find out if you can choose different strategies within your accounts.

- Determine whether the chosen target date fund is appropriate for your circumstances.

4

WHY DIVERSIFICATION FAILS

Mark Cuban, the well-known owner of the Dallas Mavericks and investor on ABC's reality TV show *Shark Tank* said in a 2011 *Wall Street Journal* video interview that "diversification is for idiots" (WSJ.COM, 2011) and had more direct choice words for the Buy-and-Hold methodology. The context of that comment had more to do with Cuban's thoughts around how individual investors can't diversify enough to substitute for knowledge. But is the statement more true than false when it comes to the idea of diversification as a way to lesson or eliminate risk in investing?

Risk with regard to investing is often thought of as diversifiable risk and systematic market risk. Diversifiable risk is the idea that instead of having just a few things in a portfolio, why not spread the risk enough so that one stock cratering doesn't bring down the whole ship. Single stock risk is real and when we think about large gap downs from close to open, more often than not, it revolves around an earnings report. Other times, as it might be for medical companies, a Federal Drug Administration (FDA) approval on a new drug. Everyone remembers Enron, which turned out to be a house of cards. There wouldn't be much pushback on the increased risk of just holding a few names.

One of the benefits often touted for building well-diversified portfolios is that when one holds investments that are not all highly correlated, if one sells off, the other theoretically will reduce

risk by holding or increasing in value. At the least not going down
quite as much. Single stock risk is one great example that investors
try to avoid. Say a portfolio consists of only a single security. If
sudden news should come out, the CEO gets arrested, they badly
miss earnings and forecasts are dismal going forward, that one
stock can get hammered lower even if the market moves higher.
Diversification looks to hold many securities to spread the risk and
smooth out volatility. Some point to building portfolios with at
least 20 different names.

Others (Brigham, Ehrhardt, 2014), explain that going from a
single security to 40 can bring the expected standard deviation
or volatility from 35% down to 20% but anything more would
have diminished returns. Investors who hold broad market index
exchange-traded funds already achieve diversification as with one
tradeable security they own many stocks. A question that often
comes up is does diversification alone really reduce risk? In 2008,
not really when we think about equities. Bonds did provide an
anchor, but as we will discuss in the next chapter, they most likely
won't yield anything going forward.

Classic diversification has at times been misunderstood. Just
owning a bunch of different stocks or mutual funds doesn't exactly
always meet the definition. One time when speaking to a group we
were doing a version of Jim Cramer's "Am I Diversified?" where
people came up to the microphone and named off 10 individual
stock names they held and myself along with the crowd would do
a quick review. Jim Cramer on his CNBC *Mad Money* show used
to take callers and seemed like a good exercise to get the audience
involved. This was also a time prior to exchange-traded funds'
exceedingly dominant role as a percentage of assets. In other
words, investors still held more individual names. Most people in
the audience had diversified single stock risk away across industries and sectors fairly well. Of course I remember one member of
the audience saying they owned 20 different stocks, although they
were all Chinese Internet-related companies. One of the things that
came up was investors who just held mutual funds. As we typed in

the symbols what was interesting was how people realized that even though they held a group of funds, they had so much overlap that their benefit as far as diversification really wasn't there. Even today, chances are that if you own some exchange-traded fund or mutual funds, it holds stocks that overlap across funds. Meaning more mutual funds or ETFs don't mean more diversification.

4.1. ARE THERE TOO MANY CONCENTRATED ASSETS IN EXCHANGE-TRADED FUNDS?

The trend of individual investors basically all holding the same stocks through exchange-traded funds is only rising. Between 2003 and 2016, assets in global exchange-traded funds has increased from $204 Billion to over $3.4 Trillion (Statista.com, N.D.). Many passively managed funds simply invest to mimic an underlying index. Recently there has been some rumblings about whether a greater (and rising) percentage of investment dollars concentrated in passive exchange-traded funds is increasing risk. Basically, the argument is if people no longer invest in individual stocks and only in index based ETFs, then the companies which have the highest weights just keep getting more and more dollars. This creates a self-fulfilling prophecy where valuations can remain high and maintain the weighting. Early on, the idea was individual stock investors, including institutions would perform analysis and reward or punish companies whose price discovery would pass through to indexes.

The fear is if so much money is simply in passive index funds then the remaining percentage capital wouldn't be able to have enough pull to right size the underlying valuations. During selloffs or crashes, investors at larger and larger percent of the market would exacerbate downward moves since every issue at its representative weighting would have to be sold, thus depressing prices much more rapidly. The other issue is that companies, especially ones that straddle different exchange-traded funds, might have more weighting or concentration and therefore effect on individuals' portfolios that many people realize. Consider Table 9, which shows the weighting of the top companies within the SPY and QQQ.

You can see that if investors own both of these split 50/50 in a portfolio Apple would represent about 16.4% of their entire portfolio. Now throw in a bunch of other mutual funds and exchange-traded funds that also might hold Apple and you can see how a portfolio might be more concentrated that one might actually believe.

This isn't to say exchange-traded funds should not be used. Quite the contrary. But diversification alone doesn't materially cut systematic market risk. And for the reasons outlined above, we may see future drawdowns more severe and more highly correlated

---

Table 9. Weighting of Companies within SPY and QQQ Exchange-Traded Funds, August 2017.

QQQ	Percentage Weight	SPY	Percentage Weight
Apple Inc	12.43%	Apple Inc	3.96%
Microsoft Corp	8.36%	Microsoft Inc	2.68%
Amazon.com Inc	6.82%	Facebook Inc A	1.90%
Facebook Inc A	5.94%	Amazon.com Inc	1.82%
Alphabet Inc C	4.79%	Johnson & Johnson	1.72%
Alphabet Inc A	4.18%	Berkshire Hathaway Inc B	1.63%
Comcast Corp Class A	2.87%	JP Morgan Chase Inc	1.54%
Intel Corp	2.43%	Exxon Mobile Corp	1.54%
Cisco Systems Inc	2.30%	Alphabet Inc A	1.33%
Amgen Inc	1.85%	Alphabet Inc C	1.31%

Data Source: Powershares & IShares.

because of the over investment in exchange-traded funds. As we will explore later owning broad-based exchange-traded funds either on their own or synthetically with options can provide more meaningful downside protection than just believing or hoping that things that are generally non-correlated in good times continue during selloffs and bear markets.

4.2. CLASSIC ASSET ALLOCATION MODELS

When we think about a basic asset allocation, it starts with some percentage in stocks and some in fixed income. The amount in each basket depends on an investors age and risk tolerance traditionally. Someone seeking only income and in the drawdown phase might have used 100% bonds. A younger or aggressive investor might go all the way up to 100% stocks sometimes. Looking at Figure 2, we can see sample allocations (Table 10).

Table 10. Traditional Asset Allocation Between Stocks and Fixed Income.

Allocation Type	Stocks (%)	Bonds (%)
Aggressive growth	100	0
Aggressive growth	90	10
Growth	80	20
Growth	70	30
Balanced	60	40
Balanced	50	50
Balanced	40	60
Income	30	70
Income	20	80
Income	10	90
Income	0	100

4.3. HOW ABOUT DIVERSIFYING THROUGH SECTORS AND REGIONS?

Bonds have historically given off a yield while providing some non-correlation in times of market stress. They also have benefited from a historic bull market run. On the equity side, many will suggest branching beyond U.S. Large Cap. The stock portion might contain large, mid, and small caps. International investments became more easily accessed via mutual funds and later ETFs. Adding developed and emerging markets offered the lure of higher growth. Perhaps if the United States slowed down, other areas of the world would still offer higher returns. In large enough portfolios, various country funds could be added. Even commodity funds let investors put pieces of the portfolio in gold, silver, and oil. The idea is not that everything moves in the same direction all the time. Some people put pieces across the various sectors of the market. Yet, when markets sell-off and correct, a lot of the diversified holdings go down. Consider the Sector Spyders exchange-traded funds compared to the S&P 500 Index in Table 3 during the peak-to-trough period October 2007 to March of 2009 (Table 11).

Certainly, the way the crises played out financials took the most pain. But diversifying across various sectors still saw significant down moves. You probably hear it again and again that a well-diversified portfolio insulates the investor and offers less volatility. In major market selloffs, it all goes down. With the rise of options, we can now synthetically create exposure with less risk. We'll cover that later. For now, the point is diversification works until it doesn't. So, what about sprinkling investments around various world regions? Figure 3 highlights the same peak to trough October 2007 through March 2009 point-to-point percent change (Table 12).

The various ETFs from Ishares covering international areas all were down significantly peak to trough. All but one was down lower than the S&P 500 Index. This to be clear is not an indictment whatsoever on Ishares broad and robust offering of

Table 11. Peak-to-Trough Sector ETFs Percent Change 2007–2009 versus SPY.

	Symbol	Percent Change
S&P 500	SPY	−56.5
Financials	XLF	−82.5
Health care	XLV	−39.7
Industrials	XLI	−63.3
Consumer discretionary	XLY	−57.6
Consumer staples	XLP	−30.6
Materials	XLB	−58.2
Technology	XLK	−52.2
Utilities	XLU	−44.9
Energy	XLE	−48.8

Data Source: Yahoo Finance.

Table 12. International ETF Performance October 2007–March 2009.

Description	Symbol	Percent Change
MSCI Japan	EWJ	−52.7
China large cap	FXI	−63.0
MSCI emerging markets	EEM	−60.7
MSCI EAFE International	EFA	−62.4
Europe	IEV	−64.6
MSCI Australia	EWA	−68.2

Data Source: Yahoo Finance.

exchange-traded funds. Merely I wanted to illustrate that simply adding more regions or countries will not limit risk when things fall apart. Also, to be clear, this is not an indictment around allocating to different parts of the world. Today more than ever companies in one country acquire a good deal of their earnings from others. Construction of goods can see manufacturing take place in any number of countries.

With globalization, we've seen more interrelation when it comes to dependency on each other's economies. Many countries advocate policies to ensure their currencies don't get too strong for fear of preventing an obstacle for shipping goods outside their borders. In some ways, this is also keeping interest rates down. With more interrelated economies trouble in one area can create problems in others causing a domino effect. Those of you investing in 1998 might remember the "Asian Contagion" out of Southeast Asia. You simply can't diversify risk away by choosing enough countries. In the next chapter, I provide an outlook for bonds making the case that the returns of the past are not possible. But what about bonds during severe downturns and selloffs?

4.4. FIXED INCOME AS A HEDGE

A fair question, especially considering many portfolios constructed with a percentage both in equities and bonds. Historically, United States Treasuries have provided the best haven in market turmoil. They are pretty much considered risk free. What are known as flight-to-quality investors ditching stocks need to hide out somewhere and that place has been government bonds. Of course some of you probably remember hearing or reading about congress needed to raise the debt ceiling. If you missed it, don't worry, it will happen again. We'll dig a little deeper later into the debt situation and implications for portfolios. But the point is the U.S. Government thus far has not come close to defaulting on its bonds.

The other factor in why Treasuries do so well is, typically, when markets come under pressure, one of the mechanisms the Federal Reserve has for trying to fix the pain is lowering rates. Bond market values are aided by failing rates as their coupons which become higher than market rates adjust. With a falling market, perhaps an accommodative Fed reducing rates has helped Treasuries to anchor portfolios. Now we focus a lot on Treasuries, yet portfolios can allocate to investment grade corporate bonds. Both in the United States and around the world. They can also reach for more yield and look to the High-Yield space where yields historically have been higher. So how did bonds perform in the peak-to-trough period examined above? Figure 4 sees us illustrate U.S. Treasuries of varied duration, investment grade corporates, and high yield. We also will use a blended exchange-traded fund, Aggregate Bond Index, which easily could be held in accounts (Table 13).

Treasuries in our sample greater than 7 years in duration provided a positive return. They had a flight to quality and benefited by the Fed lowering interest rates from 4.5% to essentially zero during 15 months' time. Investment grade U.S. corporates and

Table 13. Bond Ishares ETF Sample Performance October 2007–March 2009.

Description	Symbol	Percent Change
1–3 year treasury bond	SHY	+3.73
7–10 year treasury bond	IEF	+13.55
20+ year treasury bond	TLT	+17.65
Core U.S. aggregate bond	AGG	+0.57
Investment grade corp bond	LQD	−13.55
High-yield corp bond	HYG	−40.9

Data Source: Yahoo Finance.

high yield sold off. The latter more significantly. The aggregate core U.S. bond allocation was up marginally. The traditional pie chart holding a combination of equities like the SPY ETF and treasuries would have experienced less of a drawdown at the trough of the market lows. The problem though moving forward is bonds are not paying anything on their annual coupons. Interest rates have remained low since the Great Recession.

While their utility in classic portfolios is well documented, moving forward their low yields will make their holding opportunity cost in the portfolio adverse for investors in that key range pre-and post-retirement from reaching their targets. Thinking about the best performing exchange trade fund in our list, the 20-Year Treasury ETF, this would be extremely sensitive to changes in rates. Remember if rates do rise and investors are holding long-dated United States treasuries, they may suffer market value losses. While interest rates may not spike, and they very well may, holding in this meager low rate range for the next decade as the last will put severe pressure to generate real returns. We will examined why bonds will be hard pressed to ever duplicate the unbelievable run they have been.

4.5. DIVERSIFICATION DURING SHORT-TERM MARKET CORRECTIONS

When markets come under pressure, some might wonder if only the most severe corrections see everything more or less become highly correlated to the downside. Consider the selloff in August of 2015, which saw values drop sharply over several days (Table 14).

The very time you need diversification to work the most, it may breakdown as assets become more and more correlated, especially during market declines. The other challenge is markets around the globe are becoming more correlated (Businessinsider.com, 2016), meaning a selloff in one market bleeds into others. In 1998,

**Table 14. Percent Change Sector ETFs versus SPY 8/18/15 to
8/24/15.**

	Symbol	Percent Change
S&P 500	SPY	−9.73
Financials	XLF	−10.40
Health care	XLV	−9.71
Industrials	XLI	−9.13
Consumer discretionary	XLY	−9.84
Consumer staples	XLP	−7.83
Materials	XLB	−9.41
Technology	XLK	−10.1
Utilities	XLU	−5.06
Energy	XLE	−13.2

Data Source: Yahoo Finance.

the "Asian Contagion" started in Southeast Asia and caused a rumble across the world that caused issues in Europe and the United States as well.

4.6. DIVIDEND STOCKS AS A HEDGE?

While not a pure classic diversification move, there are many investors that choose to put money into high-dividend stocks. The reason often stated is that the dividend gives them a buffer against the downside and even during flat markets, at least they are still receiving the dividend. The thought also is that stodgy dividend paying stocks are not as volatile as the more growth-oriented issues. Once again though when things get bad enough buying high-dividend stocks is only a soft hedge. A strategy that has been around for some time involves buying the highest paying dividend stocks in the Dow Jones Index.

The reasoning is that when a dividend stays relatively fixed, or increases, as a stock price moves lower, its dividend yield moves higher since it is calculated using the dividend by the stock price. As in Figure 20 we can see the final annual returns using the companies listed within the "Dogs of the Dow" strategy (Templeton, 2009).

I first heard about this strategy in the 1994. I actually like the general premise in that it requires investors to buy the most beaten down companies of the Dow Jones, which translates into buying the ones with the highest dividend yield. You get the dividend (assuming it continues) and theoretically any appreciation as assets rotate within the index membership. But as you can see above, they only softened the downside. While some might say 2008 was extraordinary and this includes a few companies that required a government bailout, moving forward there is another risk to dividend stocks.

Considering how low-interest rates have been post-financial crisis, many investors have piled into dividend stocks looking for yield. As of mid-year, 2017, many had high valuations. Utilities as a sector was trading at a near 33 price to earnings ratio or PE at the end of the third quarter of 2017.

Dividend stocks may also see some rotation out, should interest rates begin to rise or spike. In this regard, like fixed income, dividend stocks do hold some interest rate risk. The reason is that if an investor can find a much safer government bond that is yielding the same as a company, why not use the bond instead. It is without a doubt a crowded trade. Investing in high-dividend stocks alone does not include a hard floor to protect against the downside. Preferred stocks also have the problem of rising interest rates since typically they pay a fixed dividend but do not have the maturity date like an individual bond would.

The idea of diversification is good in that too much concentration can open up investors to single stock events. Typically, systematic market risk cannot be cured by diversification alone. Providing meaningful downside protection only works when it works. In many instances, it becomes more of a hope that it works.

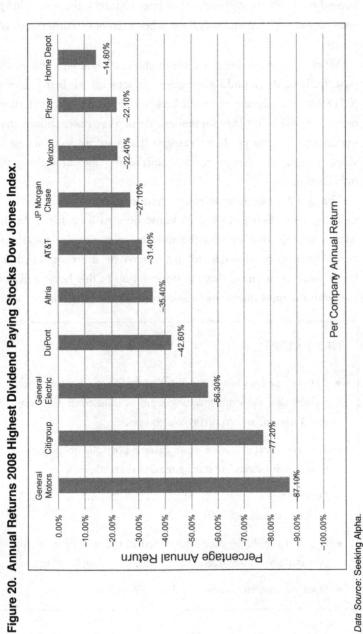

Figure 20. Annual Returns 2008 Highest Dividend Paying Stocks Dow Jones Index.

Data Source: Seeking Alpha.

If 2008 taught us anything it was that however well-intentioned diversified portfolios were, they may break down when they are needed most. As we will explore in later chapters, there is a difference between a hard and soft floor when it comes to downside risk protection.

Moving forward, there are more choices available than in the past. Individuals can add alternative investments to their personal pie charts. Introducing the right hedging strategies that will allow one to capitalize on those unbelievable market runs, should they materialize. Putting in place strategies than can produce income in sideways markets. No longer is simply doing the same thing the only choice.

The good news is now more than ever retail investors have more options. You just need to know how to look for it. In the past, strategies that opened the universe past simply stocks and bonds were only available to institutions or those qualified for hedge funds. If nothing else, the information in this book will arm you with the right questions to ask around your portfolios.

NEXT STEPS

• Get an analysis on your total portfolio to see what the weighting is regarding sectors, regions, industries, asset classes, duration, and company weightings.

• Perform a stress test on your current portfolio to determine how holdings may act during market corrections.

• Determine the sensitivity of your fixed income or bond-like holdings to interest rates.

• If you are holding exchange-traded funds or mutual funds, evaluate how much overlap is present regarding holdings.

• Does your portfolio offer hard or soft floors?

5

WHAT IF WE GO SIDEWAYS OR DOWN?

Sure, most people have been told that markets always move higher in the long term. That corrections or bear markets should be rode out as surely they will recover. But for those planning for retirement, when that happens matters. Those trying to top off their net worth to increase their living standards in retirement can't afford years of sideways action, much less severe corrections. Cyclical bear and sideways markets do happen. This is why it's crucial to use strategies within your investment pie chart that can generate returns in various markets. Even sideways and bear markets.

When we look at historical returns, they are history. While they only show what has happened in the past, they do give us data to analyze as to theoretically guess at what the future will bring. They also show that there are periods that show little to no cumulative gains in underlying stock market indexes. The problem as we've touched on, is people simply don't have 70 or 100 years of available investment years to really ramp up their equity value. With the S&P Composite Index, we can actually go back to 1871. You always hear that if you buy and hold long enough, even after corrections, markets do come back. That may be true but consider the damage flat markets can do.

In April of 2000, the S&P 500 Index closed at 1461.36. This was at the end of an unbelievable run that began its breakout in 1994. In April of that year, the index sat at 447.23. In six years, the cumulative return was over 225% on the index to April of 2000. Then while the index peaked its head up for a few months here and there above 1461.36, it really didn't break out of that sideways and down period until January of 2013. That period spanned nearly 14 years or 165 months. In Figure 21, we see but for two significant drawdowns the index essentially took 14 years to break out to new highs.

The period referenced produced a cumulative index gain of just 1.3% over almost 14 years from April of 2000 to January of 2013. Unfortunately, even those with a buy and hold, or "buy and hope" as many now refer to it as, might have panicked and sold sometime during the downturn only to either buy back in higher. Some still are holding excess cash levels still skittish from the 2000 and 2008 bear markets. This period did come on the heels of the greatest bull market period in history. Perhaps investors are wishful that the 15 or 20 most impactful years for their portfolios will

Figure 21. S&P 500 Composite Index April 2000–April 2013.

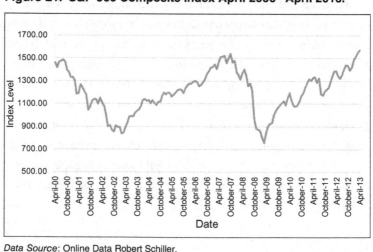

Data Source: Online Data Robert Schiller.

Figure 22. S&P 500 Composite Index from November 1982 to April 2000.

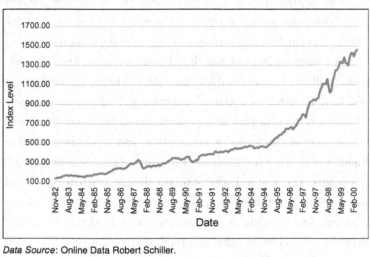

Data Source: Online Data Robert Schiller.

be one of extreme growth rather than malaise. Figure 22 illustrates just how spectacular the bull market run was for the S&P 500 Composite Index.

During this magical bull market run, the S&P 500 Composite Index produced a cumulative index point-to-point return of +958.19%! That's right, the index nearly produced 10 times return over nearly 17 years. Keep this in mind later when we deconstruct retirement calculators and think if this was your equity return in the years leading up to retirement. So, if this type of bull market happens, great! But what if it never materializes during your most important years? Can you afford to just buy and hold equities and hope? Hope that the market doesn't experience significant down turns right when you can't stand it the most? To be clear, this does not mean investors should avoid equities altogether or go all in either. Instead you should have exposure to equity markets but do so with some protection.

Not looking to burst the bubble but consider a nearly 25-year period of flat returns that also contained significant downturns.

From September 1929 to November of 1954, there was a cumulative gain of only 6.16%. In Figure 23, we can see the S&P 500 Composite Index as it moves through the depression era.

Now some might point out that if you are able to bring in additional dollars each year and buy into the market at varied times, it will have the effect of dollar-cost averaging. Dollar-cost averaging of course is the idea that on a periodic basis, shares are purchased where more is purchased at lower prices and less is purchased at higher prices. That is correct as yearly contributions to savings are a big plus. Yet, it still doesn't assuage the idea that one's base of assets would not move above their previous high water mark for 25 years. Others might say you forgot about dividends. Of course dividends would be included in a total return of an S&P 500 Total

Figure 23. S&P 500 Composite Index (August 1929 to August 1954).

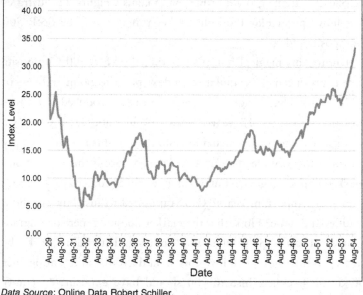

Data Source: Online Data Robert Schiller.

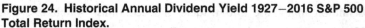

Figure 24. Historical Annual Dividend Yield 1927–2016 S&P 500 Total Return Index.

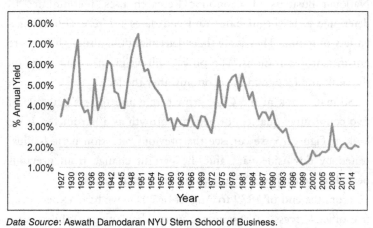

Data Source: Aswath Damodaran NYU Stern School of Business.

Return Index. Although over time we have seen the percentage paid in, dividends on the S&P continue to drive lower as visible in Figure 24.

If you are counting on dividends alone, you get more of a fixed income or bond return with the greater standard deviation of equities. In other words, for the additional volatility in an equity portfolio, you endured a lot of uneasiness with little to show for it during long periods of stagnation.

At some point in the next decade or two, we will experience a recession in the United States. Recessions come in different shapes and sizes. Not all are created equal and some are much worse than others like the Great Recession from December 2007 to June of 2009. A recession can be localized but more often in the globalized interlinked world, economic conditions build on one another and tend to bleed across borders.

Recessions typically see negative GDP growth and unemployment. Asset prices like equities can be depressed. As employment cuts and wage reductions happen, housing prices and affordability can be harmed. The general definition of a recession is negative

GDP growth at least two quarters in a row. Although that is the definition many use and traders and economist watch for, the National Business of Economic Research uses a committee to determine exact begin dates and end dates for recession using a variety of inputs. They issue their determination, although they are not instant declarations. The NBER will weigh in to put dates on the peak and trough in the economy after the fact.

So many look at the GDP growth rate and the general rule of two consecutive quarters of negative growth as a barometer. If we look at Figure 25 we can see the previous recession periods illustrated by downside bars and the percent change from previous period on quarterly GDP growth in percentage terms.

From the end of 1979 to August of 2017, we have experienced five official recessions. Some are worse than others. While everyone's experience of the housing crash and the 2008 recession are etched in investors' minds, not many recall the mild recession of 1991. You never hear people talk about the "Great Recession of 1991" because that was more of a quick v-shaped downturn and recovery. Many point to the last recession that ended in 2009 as having lasting effects still in the economy with regard to real wage growth. Certainly, it has been one of the milder recoveries in recent history.

Besides GDP quarterly growth rates, often for clues to potential recessions, the interest rate curve can be a telltale sign that the probability for a recession is elevated. A normal interest rate curve is when shorter duration U.S. Government Treasuries have a lower interest rate than longer duration maturing bonds. Since most banks get paid on longer duration loans but have to pay out interest on shorter duration, if the shorter end of the yield curve turns negative it harms banks' lending abilities. Figure 26 illustrates a yield curve example from Q3 2017 which, while less steep than others, shows that shorter duration maturities are yielding less.

Sometimes yield curve inversions are early and don't necessarily predict an immediate recession. Consider that in December 2005,

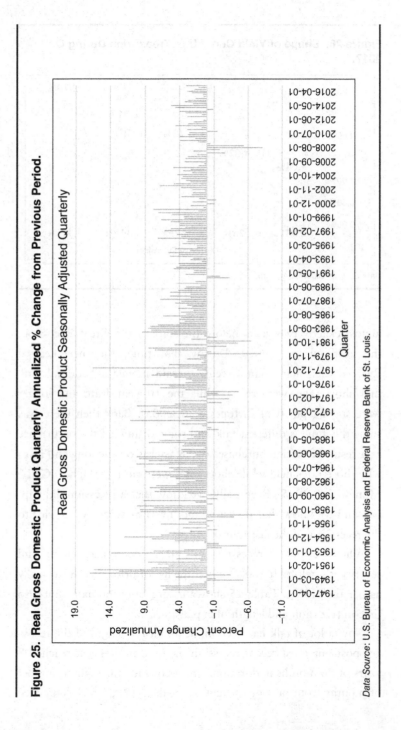

Figure 25. Real Gross Domestic Product Quarterly Annualized % Change from Previous Period.

Data Source: U.S. Bureau of Economic Analysis and Federal Reserve Bank of St. Louis.

Figure 26. Shape of Yield Curve U.S. Treasuries During Q3 2017.

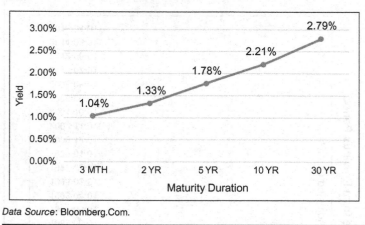

Data Source: Bloomberg.Com.

almost exactly two years before the start of the Great Recession, the yield curve inverted. During that time, the then Federal Reserve Chairman Alan Greenspan said it was a "conundrum" that short rates were rising while the 10-Year Rate and longer were staying put (CNN.Money.com, 2005). Back then there was some this time is different talk and some dismissed the occurrence as a result of foreign purchases of Treasuries on the long end as to why those rates held while short rates were running higher (CNN. Money.com, 2005). Eventually, we know that a recession did happen and we know that the curve did invert at some point prior to the recessions of the last four decades.

When we look at recessions and their occurrence, length, and severity it's helpful to look back at the list of prior ones historically as per the NBER. Table 15 shows us not only the dates but also time in recession and length of expansions.

Now a lot of talk has been made about the length of the recovery post our most recent recession. In June of 2017, it reached 8 years or 96 months in duration. The record for the highest number of months from previous trough to peak is 120, which happened

Table 15. Historical Recessions and Recoveries Determined by the NBER.

BUSINESS CYCLE REFERENCE DATES		DURATION IN MONTHS			
Peak	Trough	Contraction	Expansion	Cycle	
Quarterly Dates Are in Parentheses		Peak to Trough	Previous Trough to this Peak	Trough from Previous Trough	Peak from Previous Peak
	December 1854 (IV)	–	–	–	–
June 1857 (II)	December 1858 (IV)	18	30	48	–
October 1860 (III)	June 1861 (III)	8	22	30	40
April 1865 (I)	December 1867 (I)	32	46	78	54
June 1869 (II)	December 1870 (IV)	18	18	36	50
October 1873 (III)	March 1879 (I)	65	34	99	52
March 1882 (I)	May 1885 (II)	38	36	74	101
March 1887 (II)	April 1888 (I)	13	22	35	60
July 1890 (III)	May 1891 (II)	10	27	37	40
January 1893 (I)	June 1894 (II)	17	20	37	30
December 1895 (IV)	June 1897 (II)	18	18	36	35
June 1899 (III)	December 1900 (IV)	18	24	42	42
September 1902 (IV)	August 1904 (III)	23	21	44	39
May 1907 (II)	June 1908 (II)	13	33	46	56
January 1910 (I)	January 1912 (IV)	24	19	43	32
January 1913 (I)	December 1914 (IV)	23	12	35	36
August 1918 (III)	March 1919 (I)	7	44	51	67
January 1920 (I)	July 1921 (III)	18	10	28	17
May 1923 (II)	July 1924 (III)	14	22	36	40
October 1926 (III)	November 1927 (IV)	13	27	40	41
August 1929 (III)	March 1933 (I)	43	21	64	34
May 1937 (II)	June 1938 (II)	13	50	63	93
February 1945 (I)	October 1945 (IV)	8	80	88	93
November 1948 (IV)	October 1949 (IV)	11	37	48	45
July 1953 (II)	May 1954 (II)	10	45	55	56
August 1957 (III)	April 1958 (II)	8	39	47	49

Table 15. *(Continued)*

BUSINESS CYCLE		DURATION IN MONTHS		
REFERENCE DATES				
Peak	Trough	Contraction	Expansion	Cycle
Quarterly Dates Are in Parentheses		Peak to Trough	Previous Trough to this Peak	Trough from Previous Trough	Peak from Previous Peak
April 1960 (II)	February 1961 (I)	10	24	34	32
December 1969 (IV)	November 1970 (IV)	11	106	117	116
November 1973 (IV)	March 1975 (I)	16	36	52	47
January 1980 (I)	July 1980 (III)	6	58	64	74
July 1981 (III)	November 1982 (IV)	16	12	28	18
July 1990 (III)	*March 1991(I)*	8	92	100	108
March 2001(I)	*November 2001 (IV)*	8	120	128	128
December 2007 (IV)	*June 2009 (II)*	18	73	91	81

Source: NBER National Business of Economic Research.

over a 10-year period between March of 1991 and 2001. It's natural for pundits to speculate and debate how long the recovery can last. They point out that it would need to keep going until June of 2019 to tie the record and July of 2019 to break it. Records can be broken so just because an expansion, albeit a weaker one, is in the latter stages does not mean it cannot continue further. But at some point another recession will occur and you have to ask, what if we go down for a period just when your portfolio needs to maximize and protect assets the most? What would a 10- or 15-year period just before retirement mean for potential income draw post retirement? Consider the previously referenced flat cumulative return periods earlier in the chapter. What would that mean for advancement in your equity balance?

Let's say we have a point-to-point flat cumulative return over a decade where a portfolio containing the S&P 500 exchange-traded funds just received only the dividend? If we take say a dividend amount higher than the current 2%, what would that mean for portfolios and their ability to last in retirement while absorbing withdrawals for income? What if we have a recession that is accompanied by a serious market correction and prolonged bear market. What would that mean for portfolios? It's important to think about the reality that investors may not have years and years to average out less optimal periods.

Sometimes price-to-earnings ratios are used to try gauge over-valued or undervalued markets. As we've seen recently, PE ratios can be high and stay high for periods of time. There have been studies done on 10-year forward average annual returns at various PE ratios. In Figure 27 we can see the cyclically adjusted price-to-earnings ratio. Highlighted in gray are the recessions.

Figure 27. S&P 500 Cyclically Adjusted Price to Earnings Ratio from August 1968 to August 2017.

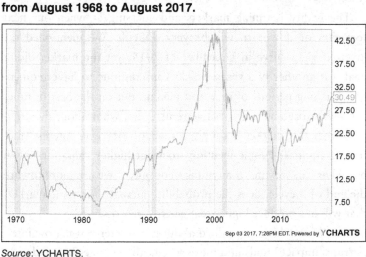

Sep 03 2017, 7:28PM EDT. Powered by Y CHARTS

Source: YCHARTS.

The cyclical price-to-earnings ratio takes the earnings on the S&P 500 Index companies, adjusts the prior years for inflation, and uses an average of all the data over 10 years to produce an adjusted price-to-earnings ratio. Sometimes you'll see a 5-year average used. As you can see, the best example of stocks running ahead of earnings was the 2000 era during the dot.com bubble. I tend to get questions around this ratio, as CNBC and other business outlets tend to mention it.

This gets into a little bit of market timing for people, which I don't believe in the long run works out well for individual investors. Just because price to earnings gets high doesn't mean corporate profits can't grow at an accelerated pace. Plus, with low-interest rates future earnings are worth more. If investors had gone to cash in the mid-1990s they would have missed the second half of the decades continued bull run. In the case of today, interest rates have distorted values a bit but when you consider the last 10 years, the rough patch of 2008 and 2009 are included and are averaged in that could make the ratio a little higher than if those really bad years were not in there. For a different perspective look at Figure 28, which shows just the earnings per share quarterly result.

The reality is timing markets and guessing at when our next recession or downturn will be very difficult. We mentioned the inverted yield curve in December of 2015, yet the market didn't peak for another two years. Stocks can continue to have momentum for long periods of time and missing out on the best of times can mean forgoing very positive returns. So, what about the argument that this market is simply a function of lower interest rates fueling equities? People mention stocks at higher valuations often but what can we infer if anything? For one, if we are more toward the end of a cycle, does the probability increase for some markets that will not produce higher real positive returns?

One of the things we talked about in Chapter 2 was how interest rates impact bonds and more specifically changes in bond market values. But interest rates can also have an impact on equity

Figure 28. S&P 500 Earnings Per Share Quarterly Q1 1988–Q1 2017 Recessions Highlighted.

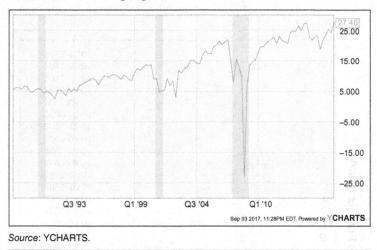

Source: YCHARTS.

valuations as well. Over the years, Warren Buffet has taken on almost mythological status among retail and professional investors alike. During my time hosting online webcasts or in person talks, audience members would bring up the so-called "Buffet Indicator" and whether it is valuable and telling us anything about the current market. I had kept periodically getting questions prior to the 2008 period. The so-called "Buffett Indicator" got its genesis from a speech he gave that Forbes later turned into an article (Buffett, Loomis, 2001). In that article, it was explained that by dividing the total market cap of all stocks by the Gross National Product (GNP) it produced a valuation metric. The total market cap is actually listed as "Nonfinancial corporate business; corporate equities; liability, Level." The higher the percentage market cap to GNP, the more overvalued it is perceived to be. The St. Louis Fed has both sets of data and doing the math below in Figure 29 we can see the historical ratio in percentage terms.

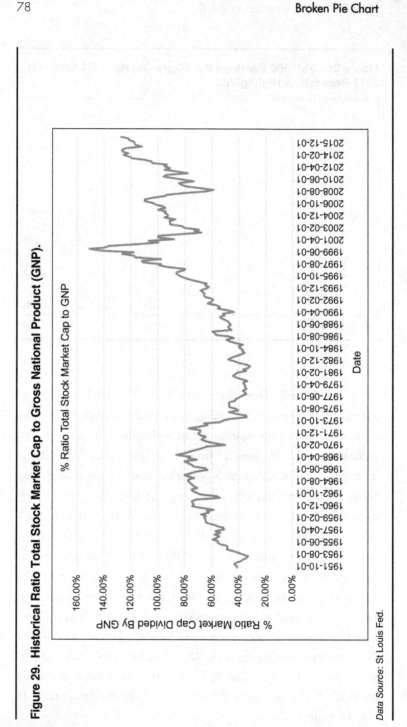

Figure 29. Historical Ratio Total Stock Market Cap to Gross National Product (GNP).

In the tech boom of the late 1990s, the ratio reached a high of 150% in January of 2000. Prior to the Great Recession, it found its peak at 109%. In January of 2017, it reached 127%. The idea for investors watching this ratio is that stocks are more likely to offer a higher probability of good returns when it is low and a lower probability of good returns when it is high. The calculation and chart does give one an idea of valuations. One of the limitations I see purely using this as a standalone is not adjusting for what current U.S. Treasury interest rates are. The referenced article (Buffet, Loomis, 2001) did discuss how interest rates can tamp down valuations as they rise due to the discounting of future earnings. This makes sense simply, because when people ask if the market is overvalued, it becomes a different discussion in an extremely low-rate regime than a normal or high rate environment. Markets can continue to show momentum as more buyers come in compared to sellers. I know it sounds rather simple, but demand can continue to push stocks up or down away from their perceived valuation.

But something to consider is with interest rates so low are higher valuations alright? Let's explain further. Those looking to value a stock look at where their free cash flow is. Their earnings are reported on a quarterly basis but analyst who regularly research companies look to project out how a company might grow quarter-to-quarter and year-to-year. Companies themselves can offer forward guidance. So you wind up having estimates of future earnings based upon some type of growth rate. This is where we will explain the whole discounting of future earnings. Those who have taken an economics course probably remember needing to learn how to compute the Present Value of a future cash flow. Depending on the interest rate, a payment received in one year is not worth as much as cash today. Why? Because that payment has to be discounted down by an interest rate. Let's say net cash flow will be received in one year of $100,000, at the end of year two $110,000, and at the end of year three $121,000. If you were doing the math, you probably noticed those cash flows

---

**Figure 30. Net Present Value of Payments over Three Years at
Various Interest Rates.**

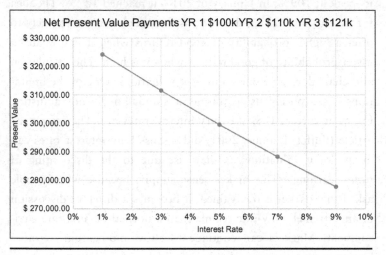

grew at a rate of 10%. So how much would you have to discount
those amounts down to a net present value today at various interest rates? Figure 30 illustrates the very calculation at select interest
rates from 1% to 7%.

For now, we will dispense with further economics course con-
tent, but the value of explaining this is that when you look at
valuations for equities and future earnings, the interest rate has
an effect on how much you value in today's terms a stock's price
based upon expected future earnings. If interest rates should go
higher, those future earnings are not worth as much in today's
terms so stock valuations may have to be adjusted lower. This is
one of the reasons why post the 1981 peak in interest rates,
stocks went on an unbelievable bull run. Every time those rates
went lower, the value of future earnings could be valued higher
because of falling rates. The fact that we are at all-time lows in
rates says another period of a significantly series of lower rates is
unlikely.

Rates of course could stay on the lower end for longer but as we move forward, increased value from discounted future earnings would not provide the same wind at the back of valuations. The fact that the Total Market Cap divided by the Gross National Product went seemingly to the higher side is not surprising due to this very fact. We could get more economic growth and earnings growth that would re-adjust the ratios. But when we think about whether this bull market will run forever, these are all factors to be considered. It is worth noting that reading this doesn't mean sell everything and go to cash. Instead, we should be thinking about where you are in relation to your individual plan and prepare in a way that elicits returns commensurate with expectations.

These pockets or periods in markets are slices in time that could go either way for investors. The discussion is not meant as a prediction on what type of economic and investment situation may be ahead. Rather it should provoke thought as to how your current portfolio would react if a varied array of outcomes materializes. People often are early even if they are correct in their forecast. It was fairly clear in hindsight well before the housing bubble crashed that prices were unsustainable and were in fact in a real bubble. Trying to maneuver portfolio holdings to time events is a losing battle. The fact remains though we have been in an expansion cycle since June of 2009 along with historically low-interest rates. While housing had a way to go in order to regain previous highs, low-interest rates provided more buying power for purchases and helped to reflate residential properties. In the next decade, a period of inflation, increased rates, and reduced equity valuations have the potential to harm not only investors but also homeowners. Generating a consistent return from portfolios even during sideways markets can mean all the difference when it comes to retiring when you want and at the required lifestyle income wise.

NEXT STEPS

- Do you have a strategy that has the potential to produce returns in flat and down markets?

- What will be your real return after inflation on any fixed income holdings?

- How will your retirement income be effected should your portfolio produce flat or negative real returns?

- Do you have strategies in your portfolio that offer growth with downside protection?

- If a prolonged period of flat cumulative returns happened, how would your retirement goals need to change?

6

THIS TIME IS DIFFERENT?

When we think about the classic "this time is different," it is often spoken during conversations trying to explain why something shouldn't matter. That we are in a new paradigm. Remember back during the Dotcom era? It was argued that earnings didn't matter anymore. That a better way to evaluate these new economy stocks was to look at page views and traffic. During that era, we saw companies' prices get bid up to unsustainable price levels. We saw initial public offerings like Pets.com which also went out of business the same year (uky.edu, N.D.). You remember, they were the sock puppet online pet store? This time is different is a way to explain away and dismiss what might be normally a red flag.

Never have we had a Federal Reserve Bank in the United States that kept rates near zero for so long. Never have we seen central banks around the world push rates negative. In globalized economy, countries have incentives to keep their currencies weak. Debt to GDP in many countries is at historically high levels. Inflation is believed to be at risk of spiking with all the central bank money printing. In the second quarter of 2017, the Federal Reserve said they would look to stop reinvesting funds from maturing securities in their balance sheet. They also hinted they wanted to start unwinding assets in an effort to reduce their balance sheet down.

Now this has never been done before so many in the investment
community are wondering how exactly it will turn out.

Central banks have been criticized for policies of easy money.
Many suggest the Federal Reserve keeping interest rates low led to
bubble creation and the inevitable busts. Low-interest rates for this
amount of time has skewed valuations of individual stocks. It has
looked to force money into investments and projects that under a
normal regime would not have passed the required return threshold. Growing debt and potential for higher rates threaten markets.
This is one of the longest periods without a recession or as some
refer to as an economic expansion out of the last recession. So, this
time is different, yet what are potential consequences?

6.1. GOVERNMENT DEBT EXPANSION

Government debt around the world has been growing and accelerated due to the Great Recession. But with years of deficit spending
and increasing costs, debt levels have been on the rise. One of the
things the Great Recession saw was not only actions by the central
banks but also fiscal stimulus. The U.S. government interjected
around $1 Trillion into the economy which included corporate
bailouts (Blinder, Zandi, 2010). These high-debt levels are problematic taking a high-level view. First if interest rates rise, the interest payments needed to service that debt will increase and take up
greater portions of a countries budget. Second, when debt levels
are extremely high as a percentage of Gross Domestic Product
(GDP), there may be a drag on growth.

Some have pointed to 90% Debt to GDP (Furth, 2013) as being
the danger area where GDP annual growth for countries above
that threshold experience on average 1.3 percentage points lower
growth. They further point out that as the debit to GDP ratio
increases (Furth, 2013), each 10-percentage point higher from
90% debt to GDP can amount to a drag of −0.16% per each additional percentage point of debt to GDP growth.

To put into perspective where the debt to GDP percentage sits in the United States, we can see in Figure 31 that post the Great Recession it is approaching levels not seen since World War II. This is important because if debt continues to increase that could stifle economic growth. If interest rates go higher and governments have to pay out more in interest payments as a percentage of their annual budgets, from a fiscal policy standpoint this could divert monies from other projects like infrastructure. The United States Federal annual budget outlays are on the surface a combination of mandatory spending, discretionary spending, and net interest payments on federal debt. It's easy to see if debt keeps increasing and interest rates should increase, further increases could be problematic.

Annual interest payments by the United States government on debt outstanding includes U.S. Treasury notes and bonds, series certificates of indebtedness, savings bonds, government account series, and state and local government series. In Figure 32 we can view the interest expense in U.S. dollars since 1988.

Figure 31. Federal Debt Held by the Public as Percent of GDP January 1970–January 2017.

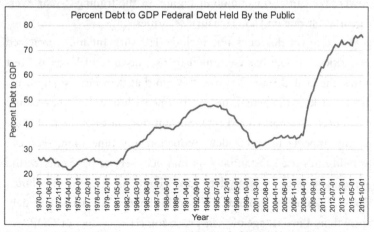

Data Source: Federal Reserve Bank of St. Louis & U.S. Office of Management and Budget.

Figure 32. Interest Expense on the Debt Outstanding.

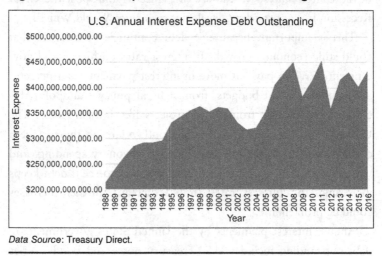

Data Source: Treasury Direct.

This does not include things like treasury inflation protected securities, or TIPS. Now debt has continued to increase year over year but what is interesting is how lower average interest rates have actually benefited the government by keeping payments lower. We can also examine in Figure 33 the trailing 2-year average interest rate on U.S. Treasury securities.

Once again this does not include Treasury Inflation Protected Securities. As debt has continued to rise, because of lower interest rates, the United States has benefited, in that debt interest payments have not kept the actual interest payments lower than they would have been at a normalized rate. Since it does not appear that there is any appetite for fiscal debt reduction any time soon, the risk, should rates rise substantially, is that debt service payments would jump. This issue of large debt levels is not isolated to the United States. Countries around the world have also witnessed debt growth as a percentage of their gross domestic product or GDP.

Within mandatory spending are programs like Social Security and Medicare. According to estimates from the Office of

Figure 33. Average Interest Rates on U.S. Treasury Securities.

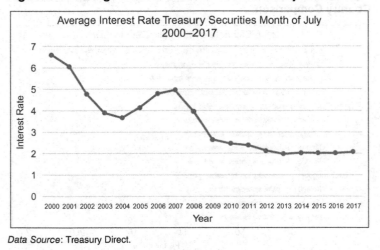

Data Source: Treasury Direct.

Management and Budgets (OMB, 2017), projections show continued increases in the percentage of the federal budget that they will require. The debate on what to do we can leave for others, for now just understand that increasing debt levels will potentially cause pressure on economic growth should things continue under the current trajectory.

The other thing to think about is what would happen to the government deficits not only in the United States but worldwide should there be another economic slowdown or severe recession? If economic stimulus is used that further increases deficits, do we see stratospheric levels of debt to GDP? Would we see more printing of money leading to a large spike in inflation? If you look at debt to GDP around the globe, we see many countries with elevated levels of debt. Figure 34 illustrates many developed countries struggling with increasing debt levels.

When you see the world picture of a cross-sample of individual countries debt levels, it is easy to see this is something larger than just one country. Of course each individual country has different nuances in their debt. The Eurozone has a particular challenge

Figure 34. Estimates of Public Debt as a Percentage of GDP Country Comparison.

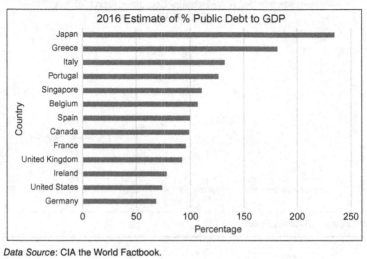

Data Source: CIA the World Factbook.

whereby using the shared Euro currency prevents countries from printing money or devaluing their currency in order to make debt payments. Greece in particular over the years has been in and out of the news where they needed bailouts to meet their obligations. It's also easy to see if there is another financial crisis, these levels would seem to move higher quickly. What would change their course? For one, growth. If economies expand and grow at a much more rapid pace and caused additional government revenue, that would be a welcome event. But even with more growth, it still would have to outpace spending to actually reduce deficits. Also, it would need enough of a substantial longer-term budget surplus to actually reduce both the year-over-year increase in debt and the level itself.

6.2. STATE AND MUNICIPAL DEBT UNITED STATES

Another issue in the United States are individual states budgets and public pension liabilities. A pension's ability to pay its future obligations in a general sense is a combination of current workers and municipal, state contributions, and the annual investment returns. One of the challenges of a low-interest rate environment is pension funds can no longer get the expected positive lower risk of fixed income with expected historical returns of the past. Many state pension funds are going to have to look at alternatives to what they've always done. Other states are needing to lower annual investment return expectations.

While not all states ratios were available recently research suggested that some states funding ratios were fairly low. This would include New Jersey with only 37.5% of obligations funded and Illinois at only 40.8% funded as of the end of 2015 (Meisler, 2017). What that essentially means is that New Jersey for example only had 37.5% of its pension liability obligations. This pension situation will be one to watch. The Federal Reserve managing interest rates so low for so long surely has hurt pension funds as many may be forced to chase yield and increase risk. As more pension funds are adding higher levels of equity exposure, another financial downturn or recession would put additional pressure on funding levels.

Shortly after the end of the Great Recession, Meredith Whitney, an analyst who became well-known because of her bearish call on Citigroup, went on the television program *60 Minutes* to talk about the municipal bond market and potential problems. The call she made is still talked about. Some ridiculed her because her prediction of "50 to 100 defaults worth hundreds of billions of dollars in the next year" (McDonald, 2013). When it didn't happen, any number of stories were written about the fact that the defaults never came.

But was Whitney wrong or just early? Over the past couple of years, we've seen a default in Detroit Michigan and Puerto Rico. The municipal market is a little more complicated as there is a difference between general obligation bonds that tap into general tax revenues versus a bond tied to revenues from a particular project.

But the growing pension problem in states like Illinois makes this
an area to watch.

6.3. CENTRAL BANK BALANCE SHEETS

Speaking of the Federal Reserve in the United States, the grand
experiment it seems will finally attempt to be unwound. How fast
or whether it is successful remains to be seen. What we do know is
that to try and help the financial crisis and the housing bubble
bursting the Federal Reserve dropped rates to essentially zero. In
Figure 35 we can see the long-term chart of the Effective Federal
Funds Rate.

Rates stayed lower for longer than many expected. Remember,
falling interest rates mean bond prices moving inversely go higher.
As we previously in Chapter 2 discovered, this had the effect of a
tremendous bull run from the height of interest rates in 1981
through 2016 representing a 35-year march lower in rates. The
type of boost in bond market values and thus returns from interest

Figure 35. Effective Fed Funds Rate Monthly 1955 to July 2017.

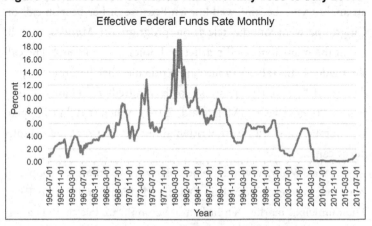

Data Source: Board of Governors of the Federal Reserve System (US) and St. Louis
Fed.

rates falling is probably not likely at all going forward given where we are in rates as they would need to move so far negative to have the same effect. In typical recessions, the Fed and other Central Banks like the EU simply lower interest rates. But in the Great Recession, other tactics were used including quantitative easing. This included buying mortgage-backed securities and treasuries, which led to expanding the Fed's balance sheet. In fact, looking at Figure 36, we can see that the balance sheet expanded from over $800 Billion to over $4.4 Trillion post 2008. The Federal Reserve also continue to increase the balance sheet with their monetary policies including the final phase higher starting at the end of 2012 to the end of 2014.

As of the beginning of August 2017, the balance sheet held around $1.7 Trillion in mortgage-backed securities and just over $2.4 Trillion in various maturities of U.S. Treasuries (Federal Reserve, 2017). As bonds have been maturing. the Fed would reinvest the principle in other securities. With reducing the assets, they could let securities run-off or mature and not reinvest into other bonds. They can also sell bonds in the open market. What will be

Figure 36. All Federal Reserve Banks Total Assets August through August 2017.

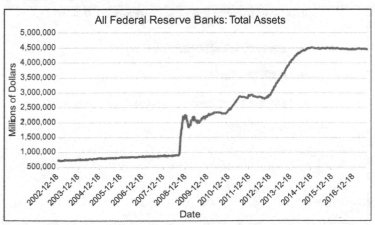

Source: Board of Governors of the Federal Reserve System and St. Louis Fed.

interesting is how they manage the interest-rate-yield curve. What durations will they target in their attempt to shrink their balance sheet? To get an idea of what U.S. Treasury securities dominated their inventory beginning of August 2017, see Figure 37 outlining the concentration of various maturity buckets.

It's not only the Federal Reserve in the United States that went on a balance sheet growing experiment. In June of 2017, the BOJ (Bank of Japan) hit ¥500 Trillion Yen making an all-time high as they continue to purchase government bonds in a seemingly endless attempt to raise inflation to a target of 2%. Of course the European Central Bank is still in the midst of their bond buying program. In July of 2017, their balance sheet stood at holdings over €4.2 Trillion Euros. While the United States has signaled a willingness to wind down the balance sheet, neither of the latter central banks have signaled an end to their easing programs yet.

The effect of all this central bank intervention is that bond yields around the globe have all been around all-time lows. It's difficult to comprehend just how low yields got. In some countries,

Figure 37. U.S. Treasury Maturities within Federal Reserve Balance Sheet August 2017.

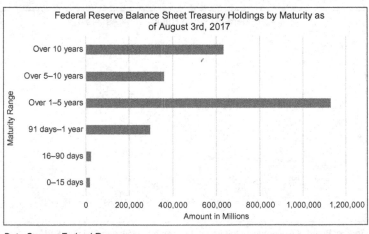

Data Source: Federal Reserve.

we saw negative rates on both a nominal and real interest-rate basis. Remember the nominal interest rate is simply what the interest rate is on a bond at a particular duration. Real interest rates include inflation and are subtracted from nominal rates to produce a real interest rate after inflation. For example, if a bond paid 3% interest on an annual basis but inflation was running at 2% for the year, we would say the investor had a real interest rate of 1%. The lows for a variety of countries, 10-Year-Government bonds are staggering. Switzerland's 10-Year-Government bond saw a low of −0.63% at one point. Yes, this means in theory buying one of these means you would pay interest each year for 10 years. Germany got as low as −0.19% and saw shorter duration government bonds remaining negative. Japan recently went back into positive nominal yield on its 10-Year-Government Bond but saw a low of −0.29%. Japan has experienced perennially low yields as they've struggled to reflate their economy over a period of decades. The 10-Year-Treasury Bond in the United States got down to a low yield of 1.36%, but has of yet to ever go to a negative nominal yield.

So, is this time different? The actions by central banks certainly indicate it is. Will it end badly? That is the open question. If the unwinding and end of easing policies returns the world to a normalized interest rate regime, great. But there is the fear that drawing down their positions may cause unrest in both the fixed income and equity markets. That there will be some sort of liquidity problem as the crowded trades get unwound. Bond portfolios will suffer market value losses as interest rates spike. Equities will need to discount future earnings down further with higher rates thus effecting valuations.

6.4. INFLATION HAS NOT RISEN, YET

The thing is though that despite all of this easy money policies, inflation still has not normalized. Certainly, above most targets of

2% annual increases. As we've also witnessed, the market can also decide through supply and demand what assets increase and decrease. With regard to government bonds, low rates in many parts of Europe and Asia have increased the appetite for U.S. Treasuries, which continue to see foreign buyers. Maybe as quantitative easing policies lead to unwinding of balance sheets they will not lead to spikes in interest rates. Perhaps they will manage the yield curve in such a way to ensure continued lending by corporate banking institutions.

When it comes to inflation, perhaps the period in the 1970s to the early 1980s was an anomaly not to be repeated in developed countries? We know from looking at the Bank of England's historical perspective on rates in Chapter 2 that aside from that period of high inflation, rates have been typically more in the 3−5% ranges than 15%. If we look to the United States Core Inflation ex-food and energy, we see in Figure 38 that after the spike period it has been oscillating lower.

Perhaps we are in a period of increased efficiency and lower prices due to technology. Due to rideshare services like Uber and

Figure 38. United States CPI Rate Annual Change Monthly.

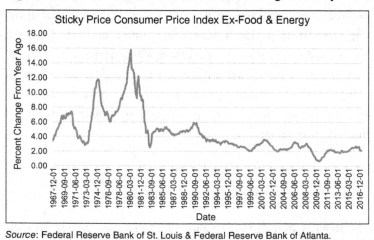

Source: Federal Reserve Bank of St. Louis & Federal Reserve Bank of Atlanta.

Lyft people's cost compared to traditional taxis has been slashed in recent years. Think about how much you once paid for a flat screen television. Go to any Walmart and you can find one for a fraction of what they once cost. Cell phone wireless plans driven by competition have trended lower in recent years. In fact, during April of 2017, wireless plan costs were down −12.9% in the United States from the previous year (WSJ.COM, 2017). And believe it or not, the drop-in price plus the Bureau of Labor Statistics including factors like unlimited data was responsible for over half the drop in 2017 YTD CPI through June (WSJ.COM, 2017).

While many items may be less expensive, the more "volatile" food and energy component can fluctuate for a variety of reasons. If one's annual expenses mostly are spending for food and energy, then positive reduction in wireless phone plans may only provide small ancillary benefits. As we also know the inflation of medical expenses continues to outpace other areas. As individuals get older, a greater percentage of expenses is shifted toward medical care.

While it may be difficult to predict future economic environments and markets, or to do so with exacting precision, it will be important to position portfolios so that they can look to produce in various market conditions while minimizing risk. We know that if we get inflation and interest rate spikes, areas of the market will be under pressure. Yet even if we have another decade of slow growth and meandering inflation with lower rates, holding the same mix of stocks and bonds may not allow for the needed growth. Low-interest rates mean low-coupon payments for bonds.

6.5. CURRENCIES AND INTEREST RATES

With the economies across the world more intertwined than ever as globalization of markets increases, there may be continued reason for pressure on interest rates. The reason being currencies valuation between countries often is determined by the interest rates. Post-2016 U.S. Presidential election, the U.S. Dollar Index spiked higher as many believed that a policy of infrastructure spending and tax cuts would spur growth and inflation thus leading to the Federal Reserve rising interest rates at a quicker pace than previously anticipated.

Often institutional money has used what's called a carry trade in the past to profit off interest rate differentials. A carry trade essentially is where one borrows one currency with a low-interest rate to finance the buy of another higher yielding currency. Currencies are traded as pairs so the Euro against the U.S. Dollar would be shown as the EUR/USD and would represent how many dollars would be needed to purchase one Euro. As the Euro gets stronger, the currency pair value moves higher to reflect the exchange rate and the reverse when the Euro gets weaker. Normally a country whose interest rates are moving higher or expected to rise gains against a currency whose interest rate is not expected to rise. If an institution owns the higher yielding currency and receives that interest and sells the lower yielding currency and has to pay that interest, the spread is positive and will receive net interest from the pair. They can also make or lose money as the pair moves higher or lower.

One of the more famous carry trades was the Japanese Yen and the New Zealand Dollar. Often referred to the KIWI/YEN carry trade, it involved selling Japanese Yen, which paid next to nothing, and purchasing New Zealand Dollars, which paid a high rate of interest. This trade had a bullish run until right before the financial crisis when countries were anticipated to potentially lower their interest rates thus lowering the positive interest rate spread. So why all the talk about currencies and carry trades?

The perceived want by countries to keep their currencies weak to make their exports more attractive and to help multinational companies may keep rates lower for countries unless all move higher in a more unified fashion. Inflation could cause individual nations or in the case of Europe the Eurozone to adjust higher, but there is potential for an extended period of low rates. Especially in light of how much all of this buildup of debt would see its net interest payments rise should central banks begin hiking aggressively. There would seem to be a political governmental will to keep rates lower to avoid expansion of borrowing costs.

6.6. HAVE LOW-INTEREST RATES DISTORTED CONSUMER MARKETS?

When a family decides to buy a house, much of their decision from a monetary or budgetary standpoint is a function of the monthly payment. The same $400,000 house at a 3.5% mortgage rate has a higher payment at a 5.5% mortgage rate. In this regard, home prices will be an interesting market to watch as real wage growth would have to supplement reduced buying power due to higher rates. The other popular consumer market involves both new and used cars. Lower rates have done two things. First it allowed a consumer to afford a higher priced car when financing at much lower rates than the historical average. It also enabled cars to move towards more higher end features many would have passed on. Consider Figure 39 illustrating the average value financed on new cars.

The other really interesting thing is that car loans seem to be getting longer and longer. In other words, they are financing a higher dollar amount at longer loan terms. At just under 68 months as of the May 2017 number, that puts the average time to maturity at over 5½ years. This is a trend that would seem to have a terminal point, since cars are depreciating assets. If loans are extended to far out in their length, it would seem like the depreciation would make cars worth less and less against the remaining unpaid balance. Even over the weekend, I heard commercials on the radio for 72-month financing. Figure 40 illustrates how the average weighted loan to maturity on loans through financing companies.

Figure 39. New Cars Financed Average Amount Financed at Finance Companies.

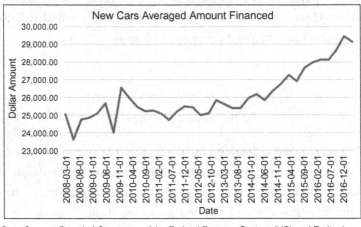

Data Source: Board of Governors of the Federal Reserve System (US) and Federal Reserve Bank of St. Louis.

Figure 40. Average Weighted Loan Maturity of New Cars Financed through Financing Companies in United States.

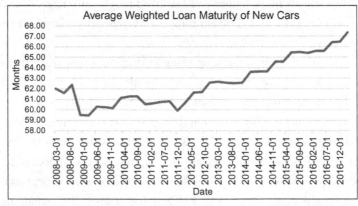

Data Source: Board of Governors of the Federal Reserve System (US) and Federal Reserve Bank of St. Louis.

I'm watching this area of the market as what rising rates would do is unclear with regard to both the new and used car market. Besides houses and cars lower rates can distort the present value of projects that otherwise might not have been given the go ahead at a normalized interest rate. While there has not been a recession in a while, at some point there will be one. How deep and how long we never know. If we look to Figure 41 we can see more recent recessions and their length.

This graph highlights the frequency and length of recessions in the United States since October of 1967. To be clear I am not calling for a recession, just the fact at some point we are bound to have another one and typically there would be some upset in the equity and potentially bond markets. The latter asset class, should rates rise, may experience an event because of the hit-to-bond market values, especially on the long end of the curve.

The central premise is to remember that we have come out of the Great Recession with lower rates for longer than anyone thought possible. We now expect from the U.S. Federal Reserve to process a successful and smooth unwinding of their massive

Figure 41. United States Recessions Since 1967 According to GDP % Probability of Recession.

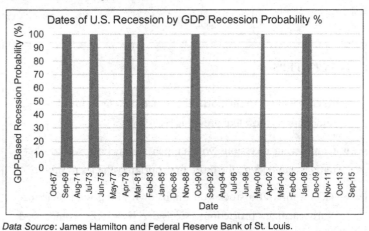

Data Source: James Hamilton and Federal Reserve Bank of St. Louis.

balance sheet. While the European Union has not yet signaled unwinding, their balance sheet along with Japan's and the United States stands at record levels. The consequences of all this are not yet known. For investors, this does not mean not to continue looking to build wealth toward retirement. Simply, new techniques and strategies may be more appropriate now than ever. Over the longhaul, markets have produced gains but in periods across decades there have been rough patches.

This isn't to say I am predicting a deep 2008-like recession. In fact, ever since the last recession, it seems like people will look to find ways to predict the next one. We may have an extended period of growth. Perhaps all of this will work and we will wind up with a Goldilocks economy with tame inflation and steady wage and Gross Domestic Product growth. The reason to point to all the debt creation is it begs the question if there is another recession or crisis where quantitative easing or fiscal stimulus is used, how high would the debt levels go then?

The thing is, when it comes to portfolios, wouldn't it be good to have things that are not simply reliant on bull markets to protect assets? Wouldn't it be good to not have to time the market but to use strategies which have some embedded protection instead?

NEXT STEPS

- Review your current portfolio to see how it would hold up under a stress test like previous recessions.

- Considering recessions will happen again, how would alternatives and hedging be more appropriate vehicles to invest?

- Take a look at a stock you might own along with their forward earnings projections. Consider how you would need to discount down those future earnings, should interest rates rise.

- Write down what steps you could take to lessen risk and still create positive real returns, should conditions take a turn for the worse.

7

WHY SEQUENCE OF RETURNS MATTER

When we think about how people get where they want to go, it's a function of several inputs. Some are controllable. Some less so. Yet from when an investor first starts the accumulation phase all the way to the end of the distribution phase, the major inputs include:

- Contributions

- Inflation

- Return on investments

- Sequence of return on investments

- Social security and pensions

- Taxes

- Withdrawals/expenses

- Years to retirement

- Life expectancy

So, do I have enough? Am I where I need to be with the balances in my accounts based on my current age or years to retirement? These are the questions that financial advisors get asked most often. You may have seen or used one of those online retirement calculators. It may seem like magic but they really just take all of those inputs and calculate how long and at what rate assets will grow pre-retirement and drawdown through an investor's life post-retirement. They may ask what your salary is and assume it will grow in the future at some rate along with inflation. Although since the Great Recession of 2008 real wages have not really increased. More on that later though. By understanding how each of the inputs is calculated you can begin to de-mystify the retirement investment calculation process.

Online retirement calculators may ask what percentage annually of your wages you are able to save and contribute to investment accounts. An estimate of annual future inflation is used to determine how much more every year your income will need to rise to cover expenses. Taxes can impact returns in non-qualified (taxable) accounts. The higher the tax brackets the less you get to keep. Later during the withdrawal phase or RMD period (Required Minimum Distribution), tax rates can impact withdrawals net amounts to the investor.

While many younger workers have doubts about the future of social security, it along with any pensions can contribute towards a retirees' income needs. During the distribution phase where investors are needing to take regular withdrawals for living expenses, there is a balance between inflation, annual investment returns, and expenses.

It may seem like a rather obvious one yet how much an investor is able to put away every year matters. So, tell me something I don't know, right? You probably are well aware the earlier age one starts the better. Starting early and being consistent can make the entire process much easier. One of the main reasons is that when we get to investment returns, the power of compounding builds upon existing investments and adding dollars to them adds more firepower to accounts.

The other important aspect of contributing to investment accounts is that it allows people to be more aggressive. The reason being is that contributions can help to make up for losses along the way. As we'll see someone at retirement with no more prime working years left can't catch up as someone who can keep putting money back into accounts from their salary.

One of the surprising things for many people is that the level of income has less to do with one's ability to generate the lifestyle they want in retirement than the cumulative returns and the contributions to savings. The reason being is someone making $500,000 a year who owns no tangible assets and has not put money away on a consistent basis may be worse off than someone making $50,000 who regularly has put 15% annually into investment accounts. This could include taxable money, retirement accounts, or company sponsored 401ks. Someone making substantially more who does not possess real savings may also have a harder landing when they have to get by on substantially less income in retirement.

A number of years ago, I took golf lessons from a professional named Zack at a local public course. I could drive a golf ball 350 yards at times off the tee. For those not familiar with golf, that's a long distance for an amateur leisure player. In our first lesson, he watched me hit all the different clubs and distances. He watched me putt and do some short game chipping on to the greens. While I could drive the ball off the tee really far, albeit not always straight, the rest of my game left something to be desired. Zack towards the end of our first lesson said, "how far you hit the ball, and how accurate your drives are had little to do with your total score in a round." Your score is more dependent on what you do around the greens.

Higher level of income alone doesn't guarantee anything. Now of course the higher one's income pre-retirement, the more can be put towards savings. A percentage of $500,000 is still higher than the same percentage of $50,000. The point is that taking the right steps along the way can help you to achieve the retirement lifestyle that supports your goals.

The question of will I have enough is a little too broad. Really it depends on how much income is needed post-retirement. During a speaking appearance near Beverly Hills California around 2007, someone in the audience asked that very question. Before I could answer the lively crowd started to throw out ideas. Some suggested you should have five times your salary by age 40. Others called out amounts like $1 Million. Someone else relayed the idea of taking 75% of salary as what your income needs to be in retirement. If that means $80,000 you need $2 Million simply because everyone knows the 4% rule. This is a commonly referred to rule where by 4% can reasonably be withdrawn each year and last throughout retirement during the drawdown phase. With extremely low bond yields and interest rates that is a bit in doubt using traditional investment methods.

The range and breadth of responses showed just how far and wide the retail audience thought was needed. My favorite answer came towards the end of the discussion when a gentleman yelled out "Do you want to own five sportscars or become a surf instructor camping on the beach in Brazil?" He wasn't wrong though. The money needed for income on an annual basis is in large part a response to the level of lifestyle. It is something that can be controlled, ex-inflation, but it also highlights how important investment returns are. Returns pre-retirement can determine what level of income is possible. Returns post-retirement can determine the ability to sustain that income. The sequence of returns can mean the difference between realizing what investors want and weather they can keep it.

Before we run through just how return sequences can impact growth and income, let's consider a few examples of how the various inputs come together to understand how you can estimate the likelihood of completing a successful lifecycle in your own investing lives. Looking at the examples lets concentrate on how investment balances change over time and do they allow for assets to last in retirement?

You might notice that in many online retirement calculators they portray needing to generate income up to a certain age. Let's face it trying to be exact on life expectancy for yourself is part wishful thinking, part science. There is good news and bad news though. The good news is life expectancy is getting longer. The bad news is that assets are going to have to last longer and generate income for longer than before. For some its more than just making sure money lasts for them. They also want leftover assets to pass along for legacy considerations. For reference, Figure 42 shows average life expectancy by year of birth in the United States.

If nothing else, you should see the upward slope of the line indicating that people fortunately are living longer. The thing this does though is indicate that post-retirement individuals will need their pre-retirement assets to generate post-retirement income for longer periods of time. It also lends to the idea that investments will need to grow more than before. Using a traditional allocation, moving too much to bonds too early may pose additional longevity risk. Large un-hedged equity positions do pose extra risk. So it will be important to use alternatives. But longevity risk (outliving your assets) can be an issue. The difficult part is what age to input in your online planning tool in which to evaluate whether assets are sufficient based upon assumptions. For illustration purposes, we will use 85 as the life expectancy date. The longer one lives the

Figure 42. Life Expectancy United States by Year of Birth 1960–2015.

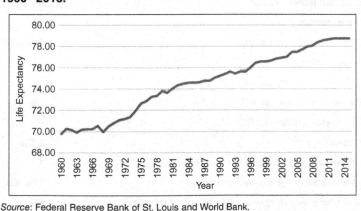

Source: Federal Reserve Bank of St. Louis and World Bank.

more the assets have to last and the more positive inputs the investor will need both pre-and post-retirement. Those wanting to leave assets to heirs should have an extension to their years.

So, as we work through the inputs, let's assume we have a 50-year-old with the following numbers and assumptions as shown in Table 16.

In our example, we can now use these assumptions to plot out the equity curve or balances of the investor. Are these the right inputs and assumptions? I didn't choose these to make a prediction. Try not to focus on the exact numbers in the table above but rather how each of these can alter whether one will have enough in retirement or not. Whether income needs in retirement are realistic. Do we have to adjust expenses and lifestyle up or down? Using all of the assumptions and starting point, we might see an equity curve that shows the investor would have assets until they are at the 82-year-old mark. In Figure 43 you'll notice the equity curve moves up and to the right until after retirement when the drawdowns begin.

Table 16. Assumptions for Retirement Calculator.

Current age	50
Expected retirement age	65
Life expectancy	85
Current investment balance	$100,000
Current salary	$100,000
Annual % of salary savings contribution	15
Pre-retirement annual ROI	7%
Post-retirement annual ROI	6%
Inflation	2.5%
Annual salary % increase to retirement	1
Social security age 65 annual benefit	$18,000
% of final year salary needed year 1 of retirement	65

Figure 43. Sample Equity Balance Curve Based on Table 16 **Assumptions.**

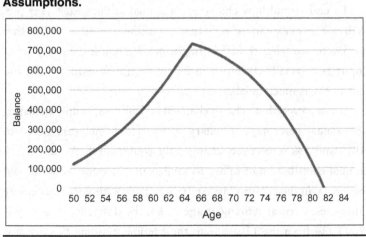

Now all the inputs each affect the asset balance curve. Also understand that these are only investments, which do not include hard assets like building equity in a house. Each one adjusted can produce a different outcome. If we reduced projected inflation, assets may last further right or to a higher age. If we increase the return pre-and or post-retirement it would affect the curve in a positive fashion. We could reduce withdrawals down to not take as much money out annually. Could we have saved more? So how much of a difference do changes in each component change the balances?

7.1. SAVINGS

Understandably you might look at the 15% example and say that's not doable. Surprisingly, it might be more attainable when you consider those able to contribute to a 401k do so with pre-tax money. This means that what you are missing isn't as much as you think. $15,000 put away would have been less in your take home pay once taxes were taken out. Plus, often companies offer some sort of a contribution match to bring up your total contribution percentage.

To understand how changing an annual savings each year pre-retirement we can adjust only that input down to 10% and further to 5% to see what the effect might be. We will leave every other input as originally designed. In Figure 44, the investor would run out of assets much quicker.

Leaving everything else unchanged in Table 16, simply adjusting the annual percentage of salary in pre-retirement years down to 10% and 5% respectively changed the equity curve. At only a 5% annual contribution of salary to savings this investor would be out of money in their 75th year. At 10% in their 80th year their equity dissipates. Even at retirement age of 65, the difference in equity is $293,934 from the 15% line to the 5% line meaning this investor would have had 66% more assets had they done 15%. Sometimes we have one-time unplanned expenses. During and after the Great Recession of 2008 many who lost jobs or could only find something offering much less in salary needed to not only stop saving but

Figure 44. Sample Equity Balance Curve Comparing Annual Contribution to Savings.

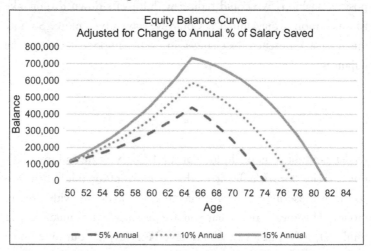

dipped into accounts. The point is that additions to savings can have a powerful positive effect on building wealth.

7.2. INFLATION

After peaking in the late 1970s, inflation has been on a rather steady downward trajectory. We covered the historical nature of the period back in Chapter 2 in our discussion on bonds. Inflation matters for investors not only because of its influence in investment returns and interest rates, but in regard to how fast wages will grow and how much more each year retirees will need in income to cover expenses. Many retirement calculators link wage growth and income requirements together. In other words, if you assign an inflation number of annual increase of 2.5%, pre-retirement your wages are increased each year on a compounding basis. That was a fairly safe expectation prior to our slow growth period post 2000. Yet wages may not actually keep pace with inflation. As Figure 45 illustrates, a three-month moving average of percent wage growth has been flat to down since 1998.

In fact, we have yet to recover pre-2008 recession growth rates. In our retirement calculator hypothetical, we assumed 1% annual growth rate. Remember though it's not how high the salary, it's how much you can put away. The reality though is each 1% increase per $100,000 of salary is only worth another $150 in annual savings at a 15% annual rate of contribution. When it comes to savings, it's the dollar amount set aside each year.

Where inflation really matters though is in how much post-retirement will be needed in income and thus account distributions. Figure 46 shows how much income needs change post-retirement depending on an average rate of inflation.

In the first year of retirement using our original assumptions of needing 65% of last year of pre-retirement salary, distributions (withdrawals) would start at age 66 of $75,463. Each year that number would need to be adjusted higher as inflation rises. The higher inflation, the more money is required. To put another way,

Figure 45. Atlanta Fed Median Wage Growth Rate Tracker Three-Month Moving Average.

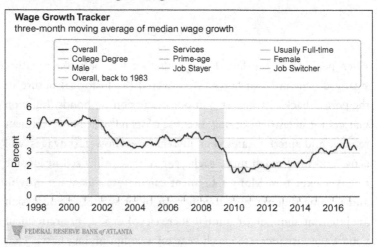

Source: Current Population Survey, Bureau of Labor Statistics and Author's Calculations (Federal Reserve Bank of Atlanta).

Figure 46. Inflation Adjusted Annual Income Distribution Needed.

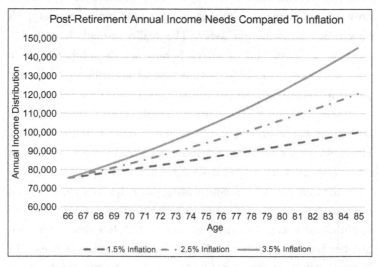

each year goods and services would cost more and additional income would be needed to cover those. In our hypothetical example, we also inputted an annual social security benefit of $18,000 per year non-inflation adjusted. Social security does have a COLA (Cost of Living Adjustment), but to help keep things simple we just used a static benefit amount which began at age 66.

Social Security and pension income, rental income, and other sources can supplement distribution income needs. You may have received a paper statement from the social security administration that gives an estimate based on your lifetime earnings to date. You can also create an account at their website and view information.

The closer a person is to retirement age, the more reliable those social security benefit estimates are. They will estimate what the benefit would be taking the benefit at various eligible ages. The future of social security is beyond the scope of this book. Many, especially younger workers, are skeptical as to what benefits will look like when they retire. While it would be politically unpopular to cut or reduce benefits significantly, you never know what elected officials might do. It is possible that retirement ages may be raised or benefits might be means tested in some way where your current retirement assets may reduce some benefits. The take away is the more you can position your assets and accounts to grow and not rely solely on social security the better.

The other aspect of inflation is that does the numbers you see released each month on CNBC reflect your own situation? Does it portray properly how your costs move higher or lower? Housing, energy, and medical may be some of the larger expenses. Let's face it, bananas might theoretically go through a period of skyrocketing price increases, but you could switch to apples. If the things you absolutely need move higher, your own inflation could be different. As we age the propensity to have to spend more money on medical expense grows. According to the Kaiser Foundation, between 1991 and 2014 (KFF.Org, 2014), the average annual increase in health care expenditures per capita was 4.9%. Those retiring earlier may have to bridge the gap between their current

Figure 47. Trimmed Mean Inflation Rate January 1978–May 2017.

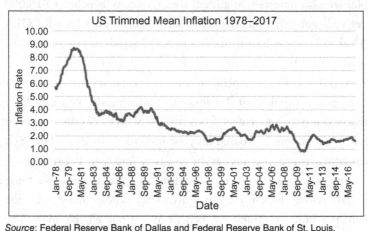

Source: Federal Reserve Bank of Dallas and Federal Reserve Bank of St. Louis.

insurance and Medicare. The trend is not your friend when it comes to rising premiums and rising deductibles.

The good news is that aside from the late 1970s and early 1980s, inflation has been somewhat subdued. Consider Figure 47, which highlights the trimmed mean inflation rate from January 1978 to May of 2017.

There are reasons why inflation could increase and other arguments on why it may stay low for longer in a period of slow growth and innovation. Inflation needs to be considered though as to how much growth is needed to pay for things in the future.

7.3. RETURN ON INVESTMENTS (ROI)

The return an investor receives can be one of the largest difference makers when it comes to growing assets the period leading up to retirement and during the distribution phase. In our example, we used a nice smooth 7% annual return in years prior to retirement and then an equally smooth 6% annual return during retirement.

The reality is returns are not always as symmetrical. There have been periods of severe equity downturns that erode capital and confidence in markets. Those market crashes or corrections can make getting back to break even difficult.

Keeping with our initial Table 16 assumptions, lets now adjust the returns before and after retirement to see just how much changes to one's annual growth rate hurts or helps the equity balance curve. Figure 48 offers three additional scenarios.

Subtle small changes in the returns can make a huge difference. We started with $100,000 at age 50 and plotted out to age 85 after retiring at 65. Obviously the higher the balance was at the beginning of our test the more the asset balance would be on a dollar basis. But pay attention to the differences that returns can make. Even the middle two lines that used the same post 6% annual return on both but simply reduced the pre-retirement annual return 3 percentage points lower. In our hypothetical example using and assuming all the other inputs stayed the same it

Figure 48. Sample Equity Balance Curve Comparing Annual Investment Returns.

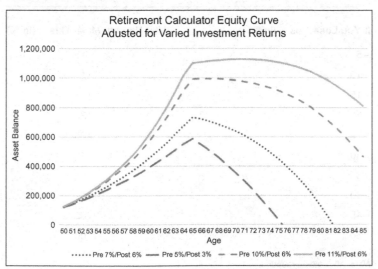

was the difference between having money run out at 82 and still having over $400,000 left at 82. Returns matter! They matter in protecting assets and still looking to capture growth and they matter in generating a positive outcome even during flat markets.

Drawdowns also matter as they can really derail the march to retirement. Speaking of which, in Table 17, we see just how much investors need to make to overcome downturns back to break even.

This is one of the reasons why even though more growth might be required from equities, unprotected stock investments close to retirement can inject further risk of assets not growing large enough and sustaining income needs. Interestingly enough, the reverse is true when investors make a cumulative 100%. It only requires a 50% loss to get back down to breakeven. The more consistent with the least drawdowns the better.

Often investors look online and see that a fund or exchange traded fund has averaged such and such average annual return. That may or may not reflect your actual experience and that has

---

Table 17. Percent Needed to Get Back to Breakeven Balance.

If You Lose This... (in %)	You Need to Make This... (in %)
−5	+5
−10	+11
−15	+18
−20	+25
−25	+33
−30	+43
−35	+54
−40	+67
−45	+82
−50	+100

Note: All numbers rounded.

to do with how your own returns point to point produce a cumulative compounded annual growth rate. Consider the example of a
portfolio which in year one loses −50%. If the starting balance
was $1,000,000, a loss of 50% would bring the balance down to
$500,000. A gain next year of +50% would not be sufficient to get
back to breakeven as the new balance would only by $750,000.
The thing is, if you averaged year one with year two (−50%,
+50%), your average annual return would be 0%. Wait a second,
isn't the balance still down −25% from where you started?
Why yes, it is. Your actually cumulative point to point return is
−25%. Compounding works for you on the way up and hurts on
the way down.

The sequence in which you realize returns also matters quite a
bit. This is especially acute during the distribution or draw down
phase in retirement. Because one is taking out money on an annual
basis, losses need more of a return to get to breakeven because the
amount of the loss is subtracted from the balance plus the distribution amount.

NEXT STEPS

- Have you estimated years until retirement?

- Did you determine the required income prior to inflation
  needed in year 1?

- What one-time expenses do you anticipate?

- Review current savings contributions to gauge whether they
  can be increased.

- Is there a gap between what your current assets will allow
  and your desired lifestyle in retirement?

- If already in retirement, will your assets continue to support
  expected drawdowns for regular and one-time expenses?

8

HARD FLOORS AND HEDGES

Over the years, I've spoken to many investors. One of the common threads is some fear of the markets. Now, being fearful is natural and healthy. Depending on what period in time the conversations took place, the fear changes. After market crashes and corrections, I tend to see more people sitting in cash. Incidentally, they usually miss good portions of market recoveries. But there is always some perceived reason not to be invested in the market. Even in good markets, investors sometimes find things to nitpick at or harp on. CNBC and FOX Business guests sometimes refer to bullish markets as "climbing the wall of worry." This phrase is meant to characterize how markets can go higher even though people perceive all sorts of these things that could go wrong.

This is normally when you would expect to see the statistics around missing the 5, 10, or 20 best days of the market over a period of time can substantially hurt returns over time. This would lead to the point that you have to be invested all the time or your portfolio might miss out and underperform in the long run. The other side might argue that missing the worst 5, 10, or 20 days of the market over a period of time would substantially improve returns. While that is correct, this would require an investor to successfully predict when those worst days would be and get out of the market right before it. Good luck with that endeavor.

Instead, let's explore some misconceptions about what actually being hedged are and potential solutions.

Trying to successfully adopt a market-timing strategy is just not realistically possible as even professional traders would agree. Market timing in general has been a losing proposition for many over the years. Look at 2008 when a large number of investors held as the market was moving lower only to capitulate and sell near the lows. To make matters worse, they then stayed in cash as the market recovered and bought back in for fear of missing out as markets made more highs. To this day, some are still reticent to re-enter the market post the Great Recession. Others are sure another serious downturn will happen, and they are waiting for that opportunity.

But this common theme of fear can prohibit many from achieving their financial goals. In the traditional investment pie chart, the virtue of diversification is preached to reduce risk. Yet as we discovered, during serious downturns every sector and market likely goes down. The idea of breaking out holdings where roughly 60% is in stocks and 40% in bonds seems appealing. Yet going forward in this low-rate environment, bonds are much less likely to provide meaningful returns with only trivial yields.

So, you have to ask the question, if you removed most of the downside in the market would that give people the confidence to stay invested over the long term? What if you could take away a good portion of what people are afraid of? The new pie chart should contain more alternatives to what has been offered in the past and should include strategies that can input a hard floor below the market to hedge risk. There are pros and cons of course, which we will explore. But for investors at certain stages of their portfolio's life cycle, owning equities with the opportunity to realize more growth while managing downside risk might fit nicely in an updated pie chart.

When we think about what makes a good hedge, it may be constructive to explore the difference between a soft hedge and a hard hedge. Often investors might believe a portfolio is hedged simply because they are diversified. That they own the best stocks in the best sectors. Some might utilize stop-loss orders to try and protect holdings. Others believe holding exchange-traded funds over the longer term will help work out draw downs and volatility that are experienced in shorter windows of time. Some still try some form of market timing where they look to determine when the best time is to be invested or not invested. A soft hedge is one that is designed to work but may not under certain conditions. One that might be based on historical correlations. There are reasons why they may or may not work.

8.1. STOP-LOSS ORDERS

A stop-loss order is designed to exit via selling a stock or exchange-traded fund at a pre-determined price below the current market price. Its name encapsulates what the intent is, which is to stop my loss. Common variations include a stop-loss market order and a stop-loss limit order. The former version is where an investor holds shares in a stock and enters and orders to sell their shares if the stock goes down to a certain level.

8.2. STOP-LOSS MARKET

XYZ Currently at $50 a share.

Stop-Loss Price set at $40 a share to sell at market.

If the price of XYZ were to trade at $40 or lower, a market order to sell the shares would be placed and executed at whatever the prevailing price at the time is. When a stop-loss limit is placed, the difference is unlike the previous one that triggered a market order to sell, a stop-loss limit triggers a limit price, which could be at the same value as the stop or at a different one.

8.3. STOP-LOSS LIMIT

XYZ Currently $50 a share.

Stop-Loss Limit placed at $40 a share to sell at a limit of $38.

The difference this time is that when shares go down to $40 a share, instead of selling at the market price, a limit order is sent, which implies don't sell my shares for less than $38 a share. In the first example, once the stop price is hit, the investor says just sell my shares at whatever the market is. The latter example, the investor says if my stock goes down to $40 a share, sell it, but I won't take anything less than $38 a share. The benefit of a market order is that the shares will sell. The drawback is you don't know what price. The benefit of the stop-loss limit order is that you have the ability to say what the least you'll take for it. The drawback is your shares might not be sold and the market might continue down further thus increasing risk.

While stop orders can be used effectively for traders, their placement requires much more analysis and often retail investors place them at areas that are less than ideal. Plus, when markets experience large gap downs from the previous day, or some sort of a flash crash event, they do not perform and deliver the desired aims. If XYX closes on a Tuesday at $50 a share, and after the market the CEO is led off in cuffs, their only product is being recalled for safety reasons, or earnings are abysmal, it might open the following morning significantly lower than it closed. This is referred to as a gap down. If XYZ closed at $50, and then opens the next day at $25 dollars, a stop order did little to manage the downside. Many of you might remember the now famous flash crash where stocks intra-day went down severely only to recover. Imagine if you had stop-loss orders that caused your holdings to be liquidated only to have to buy back again higher? Plus, if you had investments in a taxable account, you might have triggered a realized gain that would result in capitals gains taxes. Indexes and therefore exchange-traded funds based upon them do hold a diversified group of stocks, but they too can gap down in severe corrections. Plus, if you get stopped out, when do you go back in? Often that might be an ideal time. Instead it would be more constructive to have in place a structure which caps the downside and takes away the need to enter and exit at exactly the correct times.

Individual stocks have and will continue to pose risk. Take for example Disney in Figure 49 when even after a positive earnings report, the stock gapped down close to open after their executives talked about their ESPN subscriber counts.

Some revert to picking tops and bottoms in the market. Trying to time the markets is probably one of the ways most likely to underperform. It is simply extremely difficult to know when the perfect time to enter and exit is. Even professional experts and economists have difficulty in making predictions that turn out to be completely accurate or in the right time frame. Remember how in 2005 the yield curve inverted but a stock market selloff didn't happen for another 2 years during which time the market went higher. Housing continued to go up even after many were calling it a bubble. You can be right but wrong on timing leading to missed opportunities. Some might have sold out during the 2008

Figure 49. Disney Losses −9.1% in One Day.

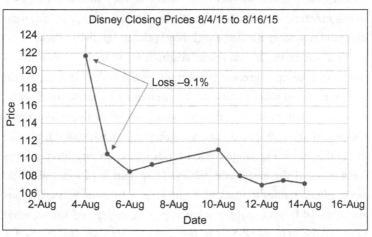

Data Source: Yahoo Finance.

downturn and missed much of the recovery. Determined to wait
for another bear market until they buy again and missing the last
8 years of gains. Trying to time the market is not a long-term successful approach to investing.

Diversification is another usual suspect for investors thinking
they are hedged against significant declines. In Chapter 4, we
showed just how correlated many sectors became during selloffs.
How worldwide markets all sold off to varying degrees.

8.4. DIVERSIFICATION AND EXCHANGE-TRADED FUNDS

Many might say why not just buy a bunch of exchange-traded
funds tracking indexes like the S&P 500 or the Nasdaq 100? For
investors in the accumulation phase earlier on in their investing
cycle, these are great vehicles. Owning diversified broad baskets
are less risky than a heavily concentrated portfolio. But for those
within reach of retirement who still need growth, indexing in itself
does not remove the downside in markets. They are great base
vehicles for strategies which are able to be hedged. One of the reasons is that exchange-traded funds that represent well-diversified
indexes offer broad market exposure. But they also are sort of a
living creature in that they are always transforming, as different
companies achieve greater weighting in the index than others.

You see, many indexes are weighted so that the larger stocks
tend to make up a greater percentage of the index. It is based on
the market cap where you take the number of shares outstanding
times the share price. A company with 5,000,000 shares outstanding priced at $100 would have a market cap of $500,000,000. The
effect this has is exchange-traded funds based on weighted indexes
hold more of the larger companies. They also hold more and add
more of companies that are growing larger. In some ways, this has
the effect of buying more of what is getting larger and selling what
is shrinking. The S&P 500 Index and the Nasdaq 100 Index for
example are weighted averages.

The Dow Jones, on the other hand, is price weighted. So whichever stock in the 30 that make up the index having the highest price has the most weighting and thus influence on the price movement of the underlying index. The market cap does not influence the weighting.

Indexes also change in composition with regard to its membership. Think about how many companies are no longer around. Even from the dot.com era to know many have shrunk or gone away. If we look at the Nasdaq 100 Index, which is the basis for the popular ETF Symbol: QQQ, we can see how its highest-weighted stocks changed over time. A couple of years ago, I reached out to Proshares who manages the Qs as they sometimes are referred and asked if they could send me the list of the highest-weighted stocks from March 2000. This is right before the tech sector imploded. Even I was surprised by some of the names on the list as we can see in Table 18.

That's right, no Apple, Google, or Facebook. Instead, Sirius Satellite held the highest spot making up 9.5% of the index. At the

Table 18. Nasdaq 100 Index Top 10 Companies by Weighting March 2000 versus August 2017.

March 2000		August 2017	
Sirius Satellite Radio Inc.	9.50%	Apple Inc.	12.43%
Microsoft Corporation	8.09%	Microsoft Corp	8.36%
Cisco Systems, Inc.	7.90%	Amazon.com Inc.	6.82%
Level 3 Communications, Inc.	7.78%	Facebook Inc. A	5.94%
QUALCOMM Incorporated	7.16%	Alphabet Inc. C	4.79%
Intel Corporation	6.29%	Alphabet Inc. A	4.18%
Oracle Corporation	4.07%	Comcast Corp Class A	2.87%
Broadcom Corporation Class A	3.15%	Intel Corp	2.43%
Sun Microsystems	2.97%	Cisco Systems Inc.	2.30%
Yahoo! Inc.	2.76%	Amgen Inc.	1.85%

midpoint of 2017, we can see that while some names remain on the highest-weighted list, others are nowhere to be found. Weighted indexes self-adjust over the course of time its holdings.

8.5. WHY VIX INDEX FUNDS ARE A BAD LONG-TERM HEDGE

Many investors may believe they can hedge downside risk over the long term in their portfolios is owning an exchange-traded or mutual fund that is either long the VIX Index futures or some other derivation. The VIX is short for Volatility Index, which is a measure of short-term premium cost of S&P 500 Index Options. People describe it as a way to try to forecast what the volatility will be 30 days in the future based upon the current market. Some refer to it as the "fear index" since it spikes higher during market selloffs as option prices become more robust as demand for protection increases. Any number of new products have arisen over the past decade to capitalize on increase interest in the volatility space.

According to the Chicago Board of Options Exchange, the average daily volume for VIX Index futures contracts went from just 1731 in 2006 to 238,773 in 2016 (CBOE.COM, 2017). Options on VIX futures contracts increased from 23,491 in 2006 to 588,279 in 2016 (CBOE.COM, 2017). Now there are exchange-traded funds that are long and short VIX across a number of different time frames utilizing different trading methodologies. It would seem natural for investors to hold an exchange-traded fund that went higher as fear increased, markets corrected, and the VIX Index moved higher, right?

Hedging with VIX products are really more appropriate for very short time frames. I can tell you that over the years the VIX Index has been misunderstood by both traders and investors. A while back, I was reviewing some statements for a prospective new client. They were mentioning that one of their holdings just kept losing value even though there had been some corrections along the way. They had a position in the Symbol: VXX, which is an exchange traded note that is aligned with long VIX short-term futures positions. There are quite a few products out there and using VXX as an example is not meant to disparage the fund itself. Rather, it provides a good illustration as to why buying and holding these funds may not provide the benefits investors are looking for. If we review a longer term chart we can see how the value has slowly marched lower. In Figure 50, we can get a good idea of how long term the value of buying near term Vix futures and liquating and rolling to the next month sees erosion over time.

When you look at this chart you might be asking, "Did they initially price this over $100,000 a share?" This chart adjusts for splits and this security has gone through a few reverse splits and the price is split adjusted. The cost to carry this long term as a hedge just does not work for investors. This instead would be a better vehicle for very short-term windows. If we view this chart during a large short-term spike in volatility, we can see it did gain in value as given in Figure 51.

Figure 50. VXX Exchange-Traded Note from January 2009 to August 2017.

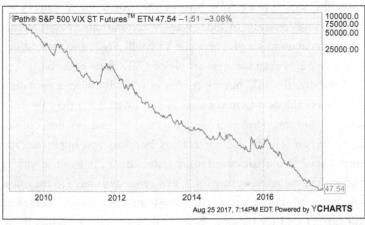

Source: YCHARTS.

Figure 51. VXX Exchange-Traded Note August 2015.

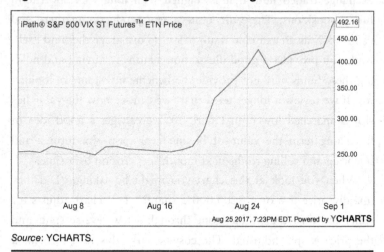

Source: YCHARTS.

The reason why long VIX products don't make sense long term has to do with what the VIX is and how the VIX futures curve works. First, the VIX Index that you see in the corner of the screen on CNBC is not tradeable. Rather it is a cash index. When you see VIX options or funds that represent VIX ownership they are based upon the VIX futures. VIX futures are issued for a number of months and recently include weekly expirations. Each month represents an estimate of where the VIX will close at its expiration. In Figure 52, we can see an example of a VIX futures curve.

Typically, the VIX futures trades in what is called a contango state where the near-term contract is at a lower price than the subsequent months. That pattern continues as you go out on the curve. When selloffs and corrections happen, you might see the curve move into a backwardation state where the front month is higher than the rest. Because long VIX type funds have to maintain roughly a 30-day duration, they constantly are buying contracts out further and then selling them as they get closer taking, those funds to once again re-buy out further. This has the effect over the

Figure 52. VIX Futures Curve Monthly Expirations August 2017.

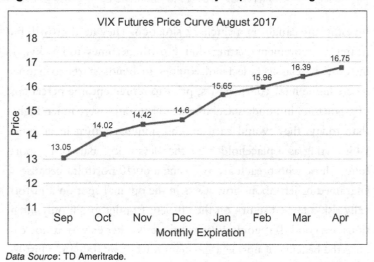

Data Source: TD Ameritrade.

long term of buying high and selling low. Over the long term, this process causes values to erode. For investors, these products cost of carrying over the long term don't provide the right benefits.

The other wrinkle with VIX has to do with their options. This is an area of quite a bit of confusion. The VIX options are based upon the VIX futures, not the cash price that you see on TV. A number of trading platforms also might display an options chain with the various months and strike prices available along with the cash index, which throws off some analysis. Plus, unlike buying a 1-month option on a stock where the 12-month option is on that same underlying, VIX options are tied to the month of the contract. Remember our VIX futures curve chart? If one bought the December VIX 15 call, that would be on the December contract not the September contract. Trading VIX options is a much more complicated process that are more appropriate for very short-term expressions of bias in the market.

8.6. PROBLEMS WITH CLASSIC PORTFOLIO ASSET ALLOCATION AS A HEDGE

Investors are caught in a catch-22 situation. They need growth but nearer to retirement getting that growth becomes too risky. So instead, the classic fade from equities to bonds starts to happen where in the final 10−15 years, prior to retirement, the percentage of a portfolio in bonds starts to rise. When rates were much higher than today, they would earn a solid nominal return in accounts while acting as a placeholder for the "less risky" part of the portfolio. Those who preach always using a 60/40 portfolio because of engrained beliefs about how it sits in the optimal spot on a historically risk-adjusted return on the efficient frontier graph only intentions are good. But going forward there is a better way to look to keep the benefits of upside appreciation while retaining the historically less risky downside of fixed income.

As we have already talked about, in the current low-rate environment, investors should pretty much expect to earn over a number of years a nominal return equal to whatever the coupon rate is on the bond portfolio or worse should interest rates rise substantially. Remember the nominal return is the return before adjusting for inflation so if the return is 3% but inflation is 4%, that produced a negative −1% real return. Interest rates, while they could go marginally lower, stay low, are more likely to rise at some point and that rise can potentially cause losses in fixed income.

8.7. INTRODUCTION TO OPTIONS

If you are already well-versed in options, you can probably skip ahead a little bit. But for those that only have a cursory knowledge of the product, we will attempt to explain the basic characteristics. Options are derivatives in that their pricing is based upon an underlying asset. They are exchange traded and are priced with a bid and asking price much like stocks and exchange-traded funds.

Typically, 1 option contract is equal to 100 shares of the underlying asset.

- Contract size — 1 option contract in most cases is equal to 100 shares of stock also referred to as the deliverable size.

- Call — Gives holders the right but not the obligation to purchase shares at a particular strike price.

- Put — Gives holders the right but not the obligation to sell shares of a stock at a particular price.

- Strike price — The price at which holders have rights and sellers have obligations.

- Premium — The price of the option.

- Expiration — The date which the contract expires. Options typically are issues for near weeks, months, and longer term 1 and 2 years out.

Often when teaching options to investors brand new to the concept, I try to use things we purchase every day and imagine something like a pizza, cup of coffee, tickets to a sporting event. Imagine instead of just going into your favorite coffee shop, paying $5 for a large cup, then drinking it and tossing it a coffee cup was an investment? We will suspend the fact that brewed coffee is perishable and can't be put into storage on a shelf. If it was something that could be stored and then sold at a profit, how would options change things for the investor?

Say you put down $5 to buy the cup of coffee from your favorite shop XYZ Coffee Company believing it was a good investment and likely to rise. Of course this is a completely fictitious name. You could lose 100% on your investment if a cup of coffee's price goes to zero. If the price rises to $10, you could sell that cup and pocket the $5. In that scenario, you have no downside protection. Imagine people stop buying coffee or there is so much supply that prices crater. You can lose on most of your initial investment. When you bought the cup, you own it. But what if you wanted to still profit from an upside move yet wanted to have more limited downside?

Instead, you could use options to control but not own a notional amount equal to one cup of coffee. Instead of buying outright, one could purchase a $5 strike call option with a year until expiration for say 40 cents. This call option gives the holder the right to buy that cup of coffee for $5 from today's date until it expires in one years' time. If the call owner wanted to buy the cup, they would exercise that right and would take delivery of the item. The price of options is determined by a number of factors like the time to expiration and future expectations for movement of the price of the underlying known in the options market as implied volatility. The more likely for large price moves and the more time, the higher the price or premium for an option.

If we continue with our example, the buyer of the call option paid about 8% of the underlying cost in this case for the right but not the obligation to buy that cup of coffee within the next year for $5. The benefit is that even if the underlying price goes to zero, the owner of the call option can only lose 40 cents. That is their max-loss on the trade. Their breakeven price would be their call cost plus the strike price, which would be $5.35. This would be the price at expiration that they would neither make or lose any money after consideration for the money spent for the call option.

If the underlying price should rise from $5 to $15, the owner of the option stands to participate in the majority of the upside, and their profit at expiration would be $9.60 after subtracting the cost for the option. Theoretically, the person who sold the option would have received the $0.40 but would have to buy that cup of coffee in the open market at $15 and deliver it at $5. If instead price went down to zero, the seller would have pocketed $0.40 and the buyer would be out $0.40. In this case, although the buyer lost money, instead of losing their entire $5, they only lost a small amount.

Puts and calls are not exactly priced the same but for our example we will assume a put would have the same 40 cent cost. If the investors bias was bearish on a cup of coffee, instead of selling it short, they could have purchased a put option for 40 cents, which gave them the right to sell that cup at $5, even if price went to zero thus netting a profit. Selling short is the exercise of selling a stock and hoping to buy it back at a lower price for a profit. Short sellers have unlimited loss potential, since if a stock goes to infinity, and I have yet to own one that did, they would have the ability to lose many times over their initial investment. The same principal applies though, for a little bit of money they could express a view and participate in a good portion of the move while limiting their risk.

8.8. HEDGED-EQUITY STRATEGIES

When we consider the three phases for investors, accumulation, base maximization, and distribution, two of the three have difficulty taking large drawdowns. If someone is early in their investing lives and adding money on an ongoing basis, just keep doing what you're doing. But in the years closer to retirement, large drawdowns erode capital and create issues. It becomes harder and harder to come back from large losses. Worse, really big drawdowns might result in postponing retirement or result in less income post retirement. As life expectancy increases and assets have to last longer, many investors need more growth.

When I think about a hedged-equity strategy it reminds me of the reasons why people initially were drawn to drink diet soda. They want to preserve enough of the taste of real soda but eliminate a lot of the bad stuff. There is a tradeoff of sorts and a cost involved. The cost is you don't get all of the upside of regular soda, but the perceived benefit is you also don't realize all the downside of regular soda. Having used this analogy when talking to groups, I know many might be saying diet soda really isn't that good for you.

A hedged-equity strategy looks to own representative positions in the equities markets but swap out a majority of the risk to that of a less volatile asset class. There is a balance though in preserving enough of the upside of the original asset class. The cost of the hedge in a strategy cannot cost too much that it takes away too great a percentage of the good stuff. One of the ways to have a fixed downside on assets is to utilize options to create ownership and participation which require a small amount of capital and then use the larger amount on fixed income that act as a funding source to reduce the cost of the long options.

The benefits of putting into place a hard floor in portfolios can best be seen using the 2008 market as an example. In the case of a significant downturn, the idea is to not participate in losses below a certain level. If losses could be halted at a target of 10% below the market at the time of implementation, think about how much more relaxed you would be knowing this sleeve of the portfolio was protected. In Figure 53, we can see the daily chart of the S&P 500 Index ETF Symbol: SPY during that volatile period.

Figure 53. 2008 Daily Chart S&P 500 Index ETF: SPY with Line 10% Below Start of Year Price.

Data Source: Yahoo Finance.

The hedged-equity strategy I use for clients involves using long call options paired with a base layer of fixed income. Since options investors control but do not own shares, their premium paid for the options is their max-loss amount. With the S&P 500 Index at 2400 holding, one call option at the 2400 strike would equate to a notional or synthetic position of $240,000. Remember one contract equaling 100 shares times the strike price. If you were to hold one call contract on the SPY exchange-traded fund, since that represents 1/10th the value of the index itself, the notional value would be $24,000. In Figure 54, we can see a profit and loss graph comparing owning a call(s) versus owning the exchange-traded fund. Keep in mind this does not include dividends generated from the fixed income positions in the account.

Figure 54. ZEGA Financial Buy and Hedge Retirement Strategy Equity Portion P&L Chart.

Source: ZEGA Financial.

Remember in our coffee cup example our cost of the call option was 8% of the total price we would have paid for the cup itself. The long option only cost a smaller amount relative to the total price of buying the coffee cup itself. We had control but not ownership of that cup and could participate in a portion of the upside but have a hard floor on the downside. The other side of the strategy is where the risk shifting happens. With the remaining assets not spent on the call, fixed-income positions either through exchange-traded funds or synthetic options positions are added with the goal of reducing the cost by generating income. The above profit and loss graph does not include income generated from fixed income, which would look to bring down the cost to around 5%. Since fixed income historically has been less volatile than equities, this strategy has more attributes of that asset class than equities.

As we can see above, if markets sell off in a 2008−2009 type event, the investor does not participate in the majority of that down move. If the markets have a nice bullish run, the investor participates in that upside minus their net cost after including dividends and interest from fixed income and their cost of the options. The ability to have a portion of assets that can participate in equity returns might be crucial for some needing a higher base of assets going into retirement. At the same time, they normally could not afford to have un-hedge equity holdings because of the damage that can be done with drawdowns so close to when they will cease working.

8.9. WHAT IS THE DOWN SIDE TO HEDGED EQUITY?

There is a cost to building in this hard floor in the portfolio. If we use a net 5% cost to build these positions, investors give up some of the upside and in markets that are flat or up they will underperform. They accept this tradeoff since in really bad markets they will outperform by not losing as much. This strategy is not designed to beat the underlying market but instead allow for an equity holding at the very time when the investor can least afford substantial downside. Some might bring up historical returns and point to the fact that given enough years the hedging cost would reduce average annual returns below just buying and holding. The problem is investors don't have 100 years for things to average out. It would seem like a good idea for someone needing growth to give up some upside to shift the risk and have a line in the sand. How many people might have preferred a solid hedged-equity strategy to 50/50 stock and bond portfolio when the markets were down 50% during the financial crisis? At some point, markets will sell off again.

8.10. FACTORS TO CONSIDER

A good hedged-equity strategy should have a place in the new pie chart. When thinking about whether a strategy like this would be appropriate think about where you are in the investing phase? Can you afford large drawdowns? Others who might come into a lump sum of money but are fearful of where the markets are might choose hedged strategies as opposed to waiting in cash until another downturn. Since 2008, I continue to see people being overly conservative because of fear. There is nothing wrong with fear as it is completely natural. But to move your assets ahead you may need exposure to equities. Strategies with downside protections and ones not built on the hope that they will work might help to allay a lot of that fear.

NEXT STEPS

- Review current strategies to see what type of real downside protect there is.

- How would having actual downside floors in your equity portfolio reduce stress in investing?

- Review your current assets and calculate how a large draw-down might affect your planned retirement income requirements.

- How would additional potential growth resulting in greater hedged-equity exposure affect your retirement base of assets?

- How did current strategies hold up in 2008?

9

VOLATILITY IS AN EMERGING
ASSET CLASS

One of the fastest growing areas in the investment world continues to be the options market.

With bond interest rates reaching 500-year lows across the world, alternative income sources are needed. Generating income via selling volatility premium can help provide lower correlation and returns even in sideways and down markets. Many long-time investment professionals are resistant to options. Yet they misunderstand how using a good premium selling strategy at the right allocation percentage can be additive to portfolios in various market environments. In 2016 the annual options volume across multiple exchanges reached an all-time high of 1.47 billion (CBOE.com, 2017). Options volume on the S&P 500 Index grew from just over 97,000 in 2001 to just over 1 million in 2016 (CBOE.com, 2017). With the emergence of computers and technology in trading, not only have institutions adopted more derivative trading, but individual investors as well.

While options continue to be adopted by more market participants, I would consider it an emerging asset class simply because only recently have volatility strategies begun to be incorporated into investor portfolios. In the previous chapter we discussed hedged equity holding a place in the new pie chart. We will now focus on short volatility as a small piece in new portfolios.

9.1. WHAT IS VOLATILITY IN RELATION TO OPTIONS?

When investors think about volatility, often they think about only how classical asset allocations judge risk, which is the standard deviation from the mean in historical returns. That would be reflective of the historical volatility of an asset. More about what has happened than what the market expects and therefore prices into models. It also is not just about the VIX Index, or buying or selling exchange-traded funds or options based on the VIX. For sure this is a part of the volatility landscape and relevant to options pricing environment. But volatility is more about what markets what markets have priced in regarding expected moves and risks. Unlike historical volatility, implied volatility is the major component in options premium prices. Underlying indexes or stocks that have higher implied volatilities are expected to have a greater range of movement in future time intervals. Something having a history of being more volatile can utilize that history to imply that future moves will be just as volatile. Other times the market environment puts extra volatility premium across many underlying securities in the short term because of anticipated events that would yield more or less movement.

9.2. COMPONENTS OF AN OPTIONS PRICE

The price that an option is bought or sold at is called the premium. There are several inputs that can raise or lower that price. Changes to those inputs effect price changes in the premium throughout the lifecycle of an options contract through expiration.

- Implied Volatility — a stock that has never moved and is not expected to move very much would have a low implied volatility compared to one that is expected to move quite a bit. The latter of the two would have a higher implied volatility and its premium would be higher.

- Time — the greater the number of days to expiration, the more time value an option has. To give you an example, on the options listed under the S&P 500 Index there currently are ones that expire in 2 days and some that expire not for 843 days or 27 plus months from now. This is also often referred to as the extrinsic value, which is the premium minus any in-the-money amount.

- Intrinsic — options are either in, at, or out of the money. If you have a call option with a strike of $50 and a price of $52, being above the strike by $2 means that it is in the money by $2. The more in-the-money an option is, the more its intrinsic value. If an option is currently out-of-the-money, then it only has extrinsic value. Options can have both intrinsic and extrinsic values because of the time value and implied volatility components.

- Interest Rates — often overlooked, the risk-free interest rate can impact both call and put prices. Higher interest rates would increase call prices and decrease put prices and vice-versa. Dividends are also reflected in the price of put options.

9.3. OPTION GREEKS

Options have a dynamic pricing structure, in that prices can change depending on the underlying asset, interest rates, implied volatility, and time to expiration. Implied volatility typically can have the largest impact on changes in price. With options, there are analytical models referred to as the Option Greeks that look to help understand how changes to these inputs change the price of premiums.

- Delta — represents the change up or down in an options premium based on a one-point change in the price of the underlying asset. Delta is not linear, in that you can't use the same delta for a price change of say ten points as it resets to a new delta after each one-point move in underlying prices. In that regard, it is dynamic.

- Gamma — represents what the change up or down in delta will be after a one-point move in the underlying asset. Some refer to gamma as the delta of the delta. It also is dynamic.

- Vega — represents the change in an options premium for every full one-percent move higher or lower in implied volatility. This input can be quite volatile as the market prices future risk.

- Theta — represents how much time value will be removed from the price of an option for each day that passes. Theta typically continues to increase for options that are more at-the-money to expiration. Options that are further out-of-the-money may see the largest decline on a percentage basis within the last 60 days before smoothing out into expiration.

- Rho — represents how much an option premium will gain or lose for every 100-basis point (1%) change to interest rates. This Option Greek is often forgotten, especially in our almost decade-long low-rate environment.

As an example, let's use a call option on our favorite fictitious company XYZ Corp. Table 19 outlines the option and its various characteristics.

It's worth noting that options can be both purchased and sold. In our example, the only negative value was Theta since the owner of a call option would see time decay work against them. The other values that are increasing would all be positive for the call owner. The reverse would be the case for someone who has sold or short that same call. In that instance, time decay would be working for them but increases in price or volatility would be against their position, since they in the end want the option to

Table 19. XYZ Corp 31 Strike Call Characteristics.

Underlying Price	$31.11
Strike Price	$31.00
Option Type	Call
Option Price	$1.85
Days to Expiration	39
Intrinsic Value	$0.11
Extrinsic Value	$1.74
Implied Volatility	43.47%
Delta	0.542
Gamma	0.089
Theta	−0.023
Vega	0.041
Rho	0.016

Data Source: TD Ameritrade.

expire worthless. For each change in the various components, the options price would see an adjustment.

With a price of $1.85, if all else remains the same we would expect the option value to be reduced as a day passes by the Theta amount of 0.023. If volatility went higher by 1% to 44.47%, assuming other inputs stay the same, the value would move higher by 0.041. Volatility can move quite a bit either during selloffs or collapsing back after a short spike. For this reason, it is considered the most important input by many.

9.4. IMPLIED VOLATILITY

When we think about short volatility strategies or systematic selling of premium, one of the most important inputs is the expected or implied volatility of a market or stock. But how exactly does implied volatility equate to expected probabilities for a stock or index to trade to levels above and below its current price? Implied volatility or IV is an annualized percentage that translates to a one standard deviation zone of expected movement. If we do a back of the envelope calculation on XYZ Corporation having an IV of 15%, we could estimate or imply the probable 1 standard deviation range (68%) that price would oscillate within the next one-year period. If XYZ is trading at $100, we would expect prices to be between $85 and $115 within the first standard deviation. That first standard deviation represents where prices are expected to remain with a 68% probability based upon an implied volatility and trading days to expiration. If the annualized implied volatility percentage increased or decreased, it would expand or shrink the area of that expected move.

Implied volatility is an annualized percentage so over the course of a full trading year, this number itself represents the single standard deviation range. It is worth noting that when I said a back of the envelope calculation, it does not include any adjustment for the risk-free interest rate nor does it include the typical skew between call and put pricing. For our purposes though, we can utilize a simpler formula to gain a basic understanding.

To take an annual implied volatility and bring it back in for shorter periods, there are a few steps. In most years there are 252 trading days in the year. If you're doing this in a leap year, you would need to add an extra day. Many trading platforms include weekends and holidays in the number of days to expiration, but in the strictest form 252 should be used, that is, only the number of actual trading days should be counted. Keep in mind though that even weekends and holidays, when markets are closed, these are time decay effect option premiums.

Besides noting what the IV is, the first step is to take the square root of 252 (trading days in a year), which is rounded to 15.875. Once you have this number to figure out a one day expected single standard deviation area, you would take the current IV divided by the square root of 252 or 15.875. Let's use an example of a stock with an implied volatility of 15% and a current trading price of $100.00.

- Figure square root of total trading days: $\sqrt{252} = 15.875$.

- Divide implied volatility by $\sqrt{252}$: 15 / 15.875 = 0.944911.

- Divide that number by 100 to get a decimal: 0.944911/100 = 0.0094.

- The .0094 converted to percentage indicates a 0.94% expected single trading day 1 STD range.

- Then take the stock price $100 × 0.0094 = $0.94 as the size of a 1 STD move above/below current stock price. A 2 STD expected range would be $1.88 above and below the current price.

- Once the 1-day move is calculated, to find what 1 STD moves further out on the expiration line would be, take the 1-day move value times the square root of the trading days. For example, if you want to know what the 49-day expected 1 STD range is take the 1-day range $0.94 × $\sqrt{49}$ = $6.58.

Figure 55 shows the plot of what a one standard deviation range would be by utilizing the same figures but plotting across various days to expiration.

The cone expands further out on the number of trading days to go, as this assumes a constant implied volatility throughout all option expirations. We can see that any prices above or below the dots on the graph would be outside a single standard deviation (Table 20).

This is a nice, clean example using a constant volatility from the nearest options expiration to the furthest out. Different expirations can each have a higher or lower implied volatility. During times of market panics, you might see the highest volatility in the front or near months. Other times, for example around earnings, you might see volatility spike up expecting a short-term large-price move. IV is the way the options market prices in what it believes is possible from a risk standpoint.

Figure 55. Probability Cone 1 Standard Deviation across Various Days to Expiration 15% IV.

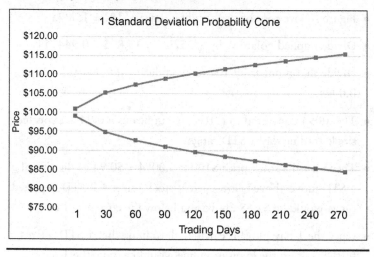

Table 20. 1 Standard Deviation Price Higher and Lower at Trading Days to Expiration.

DTE	1 STD Higher	1 STD Lower
1	$100.94	$99.06
30	$105.18	$94.82
60	$107.32	$92.68
90	$108.96	$91.04
120	$110.35	$89.65
150	$111.57	$88.43
180	$112.68	$87.32
210	$113.69	$86.31
240	$114.64	$85.36
270	$115.53	$84.47

A single standard deviation represents the expected range based upon the implied projecting volatility out to a time in the future. The area within the first standard deviation represents a 68% probability prices remain within the lower and upper bands, as shown in Figure 55. If we move to a second standard deviation, 95% probability prices remain within the bands as highlighted in Figure 56.

Unlike using historical results and volatility, IV projects what the options market is expecting the moves to be and arranges them so we can evaluate expected risk. Remember, in our examples we used a static volatility across each time period. We also didn't account for interest rates or the put versus call volatility skew. Probability-based short volatility strategies use these types of calculations as the foundation for developing where they will sell perceived excess premium in the markets.

Volatility changes will cause that graph to expand or contract. We used a 15% implied volatility; however, if that increased to

Figure 56. Probability Cone Including 2nd Standard Deviation across DTE 15% IV.

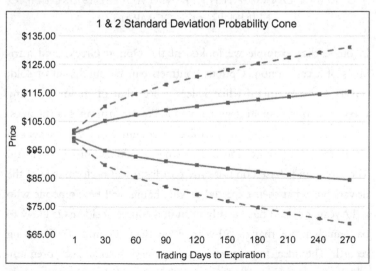

30% thereby doubling the value, the 2 standard deviation area in Figure 56 would actually become 1 standard deviation curve. The additional standard deviation curve would be even further out. If volatility shrunk from 15% to 7.5%, the 1 standard deviation curve would become the 2 standard deviation area, where a new closer curve would display what 1 standard deviation moves would look like at a particular expiration.

With bond yields so low, investors have been reaching for yield. As of mid-2017 we've seen utilities, which historically paid higher dividends, reach extremely high price to earnings ratios compared with other sectors of the market. High yield bond funds, with yields that used to be attainable in government, corporate, and even certificates of deposit, have seen increased interest. Money market accounts are paying nothing and investors are seeing their cash produce negative real returns after inflation. This is why it may make sense to include volatility strategies in the updated version of your pie chart.

9.5. IS OPTION VOLATILITY PREMIUM SELLING LIKE BEING AN INSURANCE COMPANY?

In our earlier example we looked at the Option Greeks and attributes of a call option. Options contracts can be purchased or sold. Buyers pay a premium while sellers collect that premium. In many ways short premium strategies are a lot like car insurance companies. Each and every month they collect premium from car owners in return for paying out claims if the owner should get into an accident. The premium is based on not only past historical performance of the drivers but what their expected driving habits will be. Someone who is 17 years old and has already been in a couple accidents is likely to pay much more than a 50-year-old with a lifetime clean driving record. The idea for insurance companies is to collect premium which represents a small amount of the value of the car each month.

The downside for them, isolating it to a single driver, would be if the car was totaled and they had to pay for a replacement.

Insurance companies calculate the probability of that happening based on the driver and similar patterns and take in enough premium to compensate for that risk. Now insuring just one driver would mean their risk is very concentrated. Any unexpected event by the driver poses risk. Of course, insurance companies don't insure just one driver but instead have a portfolio of many so that if one totals their car but the other drivers have an uneventful day, they are not affected as much. So they take in a premium that represents a small percentage of the total value of a car. In theory they need to set aside enough money should they need to replace the car because of an improbable, and generate a return each month on those assets. In practice that isn't how insurance companies work. But if we translate to selling options premium, I think the analogy is similar.

Strategies that systematically sell premium each month, or even weekly, look to generate income on a portion of their portfolio. The premium received is based upon what the market perceives as the right risk premium. Investors look to take in a small percentage in return each month and collateral is held in accounts in case something improbable happens. Single stocks, like a single driver, all can move or gap up or down more frequently because of company specific news. Just like insurance companies pool many policies together to reduce risk, index option sellers may choose to short volatility premium on broad indexes which hold many companies, thus reducing single company risk.

Indexes and companies are evaluated on their chance of trading in ranges. The more volatile the size of expected moves, the higher the premium would be. A good example of this would be a company like Netflix which, around earnings releases, has a history of large moves post news release. If Netflix normally trades with an implied volatility of 35% (it varies of course), right before an earnings release it might see a volatility spike. I can remember a few years ago seeing a 300% IV on options that stopped trading the following day of a Netflix earnings announcement. That high percentage implied a 1 standard deviation move of about +/− 19%. Quite a large expected move. Insurance companies would receive a much larger monthly car insurance premium from a brand new 16-year-old driver as their driving volatility would be higher.

9.6. PROBABILITY-BASED OPTION PREMIUM SELLING

You've probably heard about fundamental investors and technical traders, right? Analysts looking at balance sheets, earnings, and valuations would be more in the fundamental camp. Technicians use charts and graphs to plot price and various indicators for signals of strength or weakness. Probability trading is another method that we will focus on. Probabilities as we've seen are a function in the options market of what volatility is assigned to an underlying security.

Sellers of options look to sell individual calls and puts or spreads that bring in a net premium. If the underlying asset at expiration closes at a price that is out-of-the-money, then the investor realizes or keeps the full premium received. Often credit spreads are used where a simultaneous selling of one strike and buying another strike lock in the return on the trade and max-loss.

Let us consider the S&P 500 Index, which has numerous expirations and strike prices available. Grabbing a random day in August of 2017, with the S&P 500 Index sitting at a price level of 2446 and an implied volatility of 11.56%, we can see what is the probability of the index moving below various put strike prices. This is shown in Table 21 — the probability that at expiration, 31 calendar days away, the option at that strike price would expire worthless.

The probabilities are that the put options at that strike price will expire worthless. In other words, the 2150 put strike, with the underlying S&P 500 Index trading at 2446.00 and 31 days until the option expires, has a 97.42% probability of expiring worthless. Since a strategy that sold that option would collect a premium, if it expired worthless then the entire premium is the realized profit. Figure 57 shows a hypothetical spread trade placed

Table 21. Probability of Expiring Out-Of-The-Money S&P 500 Index Currently at 2446.00.

Strike Price	Probability of Expiring OTM
2500	15.02%
2450	48.52%
2400	71.35%
2350	83.73%
2300	90.26%
2250	93.99%
2200	96.12%
2150	97.42%

Data Source: TD Ameritrade.

Figure 57. Hypothetical Spread Trade Position on S&P 500 Index 31 Days to Expiration.

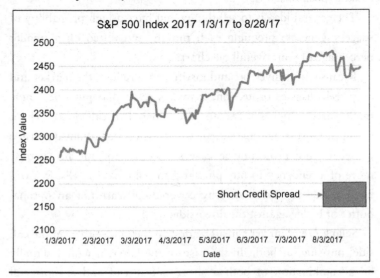

with a 97.42% probability of profit based upon the current implied volatility with 31 days to expiration.

This trade may or may not have been placed based upon strategy rules, but it provides a visual hypothetical example of how short volatility trades position the point where at expiration losses would begin. The goal would be to generate some small percentage each month against the collateral held.

This is a really important point though, whether or not those options should be sold is a completely different exercise. The underlying implied volatility of 11.56% means that strike prices which have very high probabilities now might not be as probable or likely if volatility should jump.

A strategy which looks to sell excess volatility premium in the market requires a great deal of calculus. Is the premium expensive or cheap? Do the strike prices' probabilities understate the real risk based on modeling? What is the current volatility skew in the markets and how does that impact premiums? While short volatility strategies may be easier than ever to execute, thanks to technology, it may be best to find strategies which offer a good systematic disciplined approach with experience in making adjustments to existing positions.

The general idea is to sell things that have a high probability of success, generate premium each month, and do so on a smaller percentage of your overall pie chart.

Because most investors and institutions are long the market and may seek disaster protection, it makes sense that put prices normally carry a higher premium as compared to call prices. Think about it, most of the investment world is worried about downside protection not protecting in case stocks rise too much. There is more of a tendency to buy puts and to sell covered calls. We will have a little to say about why covered calls are not an optimal buffer or hedge against the downside.

Selling premium via spread trades can be done either on the call side, put side, or both. In the case of the latter, it would actually be a combination of both a short put spread and a short call spread known as an Iron Condor. But ever since 1987, the skew of an options chain for broad indexes like the S&P 500 has shown more premium further away from the market than on calls. Figure 58 shows a chart of the volatility skew on 30-day options taken mid-2017.

The left axis represents the implied volatility percentage while the bottom is the strike price. With the underlying S&P 500 Index level sitting around 2445, we can see below that puts not only have higher implied volatility than calls, but they do so on strike prices much further away. What this means as for strategies selling premium is that those volatility premiums are more robust on the downside than on calls above the market. If sustained volatility environments would return to equities markets or if interest rates normalize, there is a greater chance of call premiums returning.

To think about it in another way, generally it is easier to get premium for selling really far out of the money options on puts than it is on calls. It is interesting that using a normal probability distribution it does not tilt more of a premium to either side. But in reality the downside is bid up and premiums are higher. After 1987, the tech collapse in 2000, and the 2008–2009 Great Recession, a lot of strategies are willing to pay for low probability

Figure 58. Volatility Skew of S&P 500 Index Options Example.

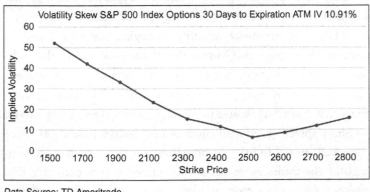

Data Source: TD Ameritrade.

puts really far away for disaster protection. A short volatility strategy looks to sell those options and generate monthly income.

9.7. BENEFITS AND RISKS IN PREMIUM SELLING STRATEGIES

Selling options that have very low probabilities of winding up in a loss would generally seem like a safe strategy. The real risk is that however unlikely, short volatility spread strategies carry Black Swan risk. This is the risk that some unknown outlier event occurs in markets. Short volatility strategies can use some leverage and this is why it is important that if these strategies are used in portfolios they should be sized properly to manage risk. The benefits generally are that for a small percentage of assets, they have the potential to provide excess returns not only in good markets but sideways and bear markets as well. The risk is some sharp quick move toward the direction of the short positions that are really far away from the current market.

What I like about a short volatility strategy, which looks to sell options that have a high probability of success, is that it provides a way to generate returns in different markets. Historically, strategies that offer little correlation to equity markets and almost no correlation to interest rate markets can in itself be a diversifier. Targeted monthly returns are the result of a long-term systematic strategy that happens to use short-term option vehicles to express the strategy.

While there are many volatility strategies, one of the keys in selecting the strategy that I use is that it need not simply always be short volatility. Instead, being more selective and waiting strategically for the right entry points can help further increase the probability that trades will be able to run their course through expiration.

Short spread positions benefit from positive time decay since they want to sell to bring in premium and then watch it erode to zero as the trades expire. It is nice knowing that each day that passes positions lose more and more time value, even on holidays when the market is closed.

Volatility may be an emerging asset class, but it should be in the new pie chart. "Hedged Equity," "Short Volatility," and in the upcoming chapter "Buffered Equity" are all ways in which investors can look to generate returns, reduce correlation, and reduce risk. It is worth noting that option strategies require a lot of inputs, calculations, planning, and risk management to increase the chance of being successful in the long term. Discipline on both entering and exiting positions is paramount to increasing long-term portfolio benefits. Using a strategy that imparts those qualities should be foremost in selection criteria.

A final thought on short volatility strategies. The sizing of this slice in the pie chart is extremely important. For this piece, you are looking to generate outsized returns in various market environments that are historically non-correlated. This type of approach can be a nice addition to a portfolio. But it is imperative that it is sized correctly based upon the end goals.

NEXT STEPS

- Could your portfolio benefit from alternative income strategies?

- Determine the proper percentage for short volatility strategies.

- Evaluate whether managers are always in the market or show discipline and patience. Do they pick their spots to increase the probability of success?

- Lean toward strategies that have a systematic approach.

- How could generating income through short volatility strategies help to produce income in retirement?

10

SYNTHETICS TO BUILD POSITIONS
WITH A SEAT BELT

The advent of options and other derivatives provided the ability to develop synthetic versions of equity positions that can shift the risk around a risk graph. Options, as we have noted, continue to grow year after year. Their utility for hedging and generating income have been covered, but they also have the ability to design strategies which can replicate long ownership, synthetically collect dividends, or change the size and shape of profits and losses along a risk graph.

About two years ago we decided to impart synthetics to our landscaping. After living in a home where the landscaping was included as part of our monthly home owner's dues, our new house required us to do everything ourselves. This included using quite a bit of water, which cost money to keep the lawn green. Putting in the winter grass and then the summer grass at seasonal intervals. And, of course, using a lawnmower however many times a month. Time for a synthetic lawn option. You had me at no more lawnmower!

We installed synthetic turf in the yard and it provided more upside than I even thought. Our water bill dropped significantly. No more mowing or weedwhacker needed. It was simply there year-round and the same constant color green all year-round. It will take some time to reach the payoff point, but not having to do

anything but hose it off every now and then was great. The opportunity cost saved was well worth it and eventually the hard costs
will be realized as well. If we factored in what we might have paid
someone else monthly that difference would be realized even
sooner.

We preserved most of the good stuff but shifted the downside
risk to something else, should we need to repair or replace the synthetic turf earlier than projected. The volatility was reduced since
the fake turf just sits there except for the occasional rogue weed or
debris that needs to be attended to.

10.1. PROFIT-AND-LOSS GRAPHS

When a stock or exchange-traded fund is purchased, it begins to
make or lose money the moment it shifts higher or lower in price
excluding commissions. If you purchase 100 shares of stock for
$100 a share, the transaction requires $10,000 of capital. If the
stock moves up to $101 a share, you have un-realized gain of $1
per share or $100 on the position. Likewise, if the stock moves a
$1 below the purchase price, the position has an un-realized loss.
Long securities have theoretically unlimited gain potential to infin-
ity and max downside to zero. If we look at a simple risk graph of
just owing shares of stock in Figure 59, we can see that as price
moves higher the position gains but if the share price drops losses
start.

On the graph, the left axis represents the profit or loss percentage while the bottom axis shows the percent higher or lower in the
market price on a percentage basis from the entry price. The line is
the S&P 500 Index SPY exchange-traded fund. The key to using
these graphs is to check the intersection between market movement
and profit-and-loss percentage. The graph shows that when the
ETF is first purchased, the 0% profit/loss on the left intersects with
the 0% market change from the bottom. This makes sense since
you just bought the security and it has not moved.

Figure 59. Hypothetical Profit-and-Loss Graph on the S&P 500 Exchange-Trade Fund Symbol: SPY.

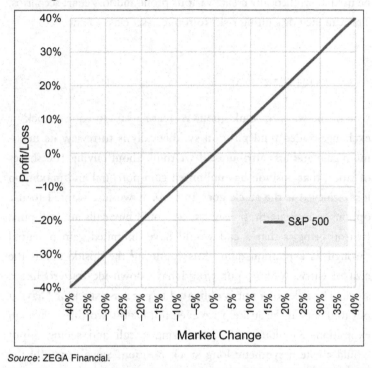

Source: ZEGA Financial.

Let's say the security moves higher 10%, you now would look to see where the line intersects with the +10% market change from down below and then trace over to the left where sure enough the profit is 10%. This is a pretty straightforward example. Some profit-and-loss graphs use dollar amounts instead of percent on the left side. Others use the price rather than percentage on the bottom. But whatever the method they allow an investor to understand what they are making or losing, or what their risk is, as changes happen to their underlying positions. Risk graphs sometimes take a little practice to get the hang of simply because you have to re-orient yourself as price moving higher means you get further right on the bottom axis and vice versa when prices move lower. Unlike a chart where price moving higher means it moves up or the inverse when it moves lower. As we will see, options can be used to synthetically create various profit-and-loss chart scenarios. This can include shifting risk from one asset class to another.

10.2. SYNTHETIC POSITIONS USING OPTIONS EXAMPLE

One of the ways to think about recreating say an equity stock or exchange-traded fund position synthetically is to review its maximum gain and loss attributes. If we think about buying 100 shares of stock, that position has unlimited gain potential and maximum loss achieved if the stock goes to zero. If we just wanted to use options to recreate those aspects, we could buy calls and sell puts. Reason being is that a call would have unlimited gain potential through its expiration date, thus capturing the upside minus the cost of entry. A short put would have downside to zero like a stock. The seller of a put is obligated to purchase stock or "have it put to them" at the strike price even if it is now worthless through expiration. Simultaneously purchasing a call and selling a put would create a synthetic long stock position. Since generally the put would fetch a bit more premium than the call at-the-money strike price, the position would generally share the profit-and-loss graph of a stock. Figure 60 is created by adding a dotted line representing the synthetic long position to the graph in Figure 59.

Notice that while because of the net credit at entry it provides a tiny bit more profit, essentially it still has almost all the entire downside risk. In this regard, it does not provide any hedge or meaningful buffer.

10.3. SYNTHETIC OPTIONS TO COLLECT DIVIDENDS

Most times investors who want to collect dividends go out and buy a stock or exchange-traded fund. They might be either

---

Figure 60. Hypothetical Synthetic Long Stock Position vs. Long Stock.

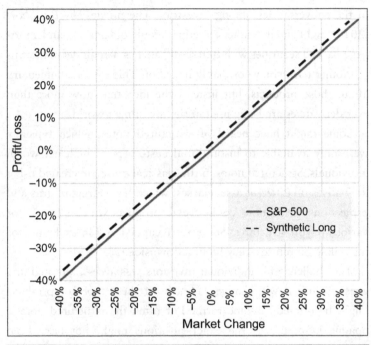

monthly or quarterly. In theory, the stock paying out a dividend will see its underlying price reduced by the amount of the dividend paid. If instead the goal is to just capture the dividend, it can also be constructed by options. The dividend is contained in the price of a put as extrinsic value. If you think about cash flows, an investor receives dividend payments that are discounted down by the interest rate over the period. The put premium contains those discounted values of the dividends. So, if we wanted to construct a synthetic position to capture that dividend we might use a combination of selling an at- or in-the-money put with a simultaneous purchase of a long put to create a spread position. These types of positions might be contained in the buffered equity strategies as a funding source and risk substitution.

10.4. STRUCTURED NOTES

Over the past decade, plus derivatives have become more known in the conversations among investors. The movie *The Big Short* (2015) highlighted synthetic credit default obligations and mortgage backed securities with different tranches. Credit default swaps is another term you've probably heard of. This isn't a commentary about those products, but instead the idea that now more than ever derivatives are being used in the investment world.

Some might have heard of structured notes, which typically were only available to institutional customers or high net worth individuals. Structured notes in the classical sense are created using derivatives on different asset classes, which have target returns and protections. Institutions could create products which allowed for various payoff structures. Some were capped and in exchange for the ceiling on returns, they limited downside risk.

The challenge for individual investors was access, although my guess is that it will change as more of these types of products might be offered in some form. But often the structured note is opaque in nature as the exact positions might not have been known beyond the payout and risk structure. Liquidity could be an issue as unlike a stock which has a constantly updating bid and ask price and could be sold, it wasn't that easy with structured notes as they don't trade on public markets.

If we think about the characteristics of the structured note product, it might have a fixed holding period or maturity date. The maximum upside or downside might be known prior to closing on the transaction. The problem with structured notes is that unlike individual positions held in a brokerage account, holding the note means relying on the creditworthiness of the institution issuing the note. This was an issue during the unprecedented Great Recession where investors holding notes from Lehman Brothers (Braham, 2013) lost when they declared bankruptcy.

These products are interesting, in that their intention is to use a combination of asset classes and sometimes shift the primary risk to the less volatile one while using leverage on the upside to create outside gains. So, what if you could take the positive characteristics and eliminate many of the negative ones?

10.5. BUFFERED EQUITY STRATEGIES

A buffered equity strategy looks to provide protection for a good portion of the downside while participating in or exceeding the upside. Unlike a structured note, it builds positions within a portfolio that an investor can see in their account, therefore offering real transparency. The equity exposure is developed using options to synthetically build risk and reward points along a profit-and-loss chart. The equity downside buffer it creates is where a good portion of the downside is suspended or removed until the underlying index falls through. Generally, options are used with certain longer term expiration dates ranging from 18 to 36 months. Unlike a structured note that is not liquid, since all the positions used are highly liquid options or exchange-traded funds, they can be traded out of.

The other part of the position is made up of shorter duration fixed income exchange-traded funds, which hold their holdings to maturity. While many people think of bonds as providing income or de-risking portfolios, fixed income in a Buffered Index strategy is meant more as a funding source to build the synthetic options positions. When we think about the profit-and-loss graphs, depending on what the goals are, a combination of options contracts and short duration fixed income can mold and shape the graphs depending on the posture and risk of investors.

I use buffered strategies that include a few different types of profiles. For example, in Figure 61 we can see how the profit-and-loss graph for the equity portion of a buffered position looks compared to just holding the S&P 500 Index exchange-traded fund SPY.

Figure 61. Profit-and-Loss Graph Equity Portion of ZBIG Buffered Indexed Growth Leveraged.

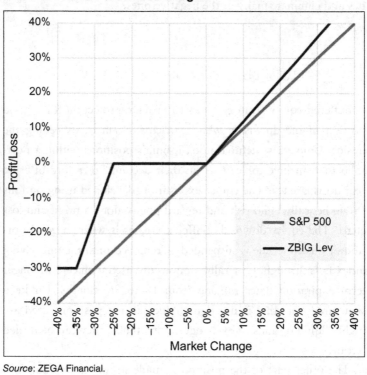

Source: ZEGA Financial.

The risk graph in Figure 61 represents the profit and loss at expiration. While the SPY begins losing as soon as price gets below the initial cost, the target buffer created on the synthetic long equity position suspends losses until the underlying S&P 500 Index goes below 25%. At that point, losses begin to accelerate until maxing out at −30%. The design of the strategy is to outperform the S&P 500 Index at all the points along the equity risk graph. On the upside, the target is to gain more than the S&P 500 Index. This is where the leverage comes in.

You might be asking, so what's the downside? First this represents just the profit-and-loss targets at expiration of a combination of short put spreads and long calls. While these are liquid holdings that can be closed at any time, this is designed to be held until maturity when the positions expire 18–36 months from inception. If an investor needs to close out early, their actual profit and loss might be different. The other aspect of this strategy is a good part of the account is holding short duration fixed high yield fixed income positions that are held to maturity. This provides monthly cash flows in the form of dividends, which allow a target for small percentage gains even between 0% and negative −25%, which represents the targeted buffer zone. It also can contribute to the purchase along with premium selling to buying the long exposure.

10.6. RISK SHIFTING

Equities have historically had a higher volatility or standard deviation than that of fixed income. In the buffered equity strategies that I utilize, there is a shift from equity risk to that of short duration high yield bonds. Shorter duration bonds have less sensitivity to interest rates. Also, the exchange-traded funds hold the bond portfolio to their maturity. This means that if bonds should move lower, as long as the individual bond has not defaulted, it gets redeemed at maturity at its par value. The shift in risk therefore is from un-hedged equity risk to short duration high yield default risk. There is no perfect strategy that eliminates every risk. But in shifting to an asset class which has historically less volatility, the profile is altered. If we look at Figure 62 we can see the difference in the standard deviation of the Barclays High Yield 1–3 Year Index compared with the S&P 500 Index.

For each year the monthly returns were used and annualized. We can see that near-term high yield is much less volatile compared with the S&P 500 Index. So, what you wind up having is a combination of a near-term, high-yield base with synthetic long-leveraged equity.

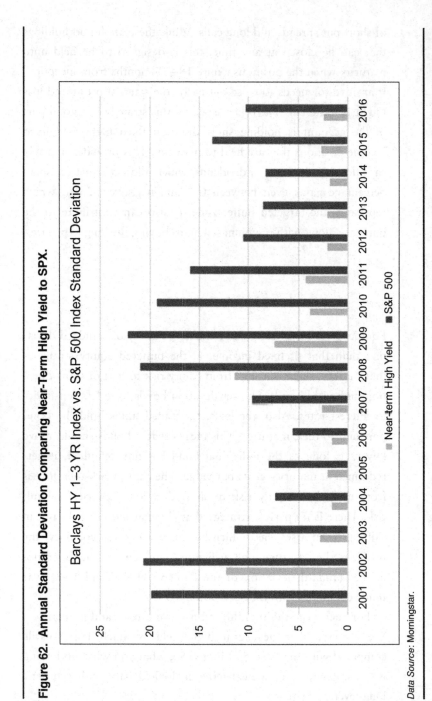

Figure 62. Annual Standard Deviation Comparing Near-Term High Yield to SPX.

Barclays HY 1–3 YR Index vs. S&P 500 Index Standard Deviation

■ Near-term High Yield   ■ S&P 500

Data Source: Morningstar.

10.7. EQUITY RISK

With the Buffered Index strategy, the target area where it would begin to pick up losses along with the underlying S&P 500 Index is greater than −25%. So, the question naturally arises. How often does the market move lower than that? Figure 63 is the graphical display of the total return of the S&P 500 Index (including dividends) from 1928 through 2016.

For an investor who is taking equity risk already, why not use a strategy that offers a buffer to the downside and a different risk profile? For investors closer in to retirement, they may be better off with more of a hedged equity strategy that puts a floor on the downside. But for others, having a cushion where only if the market sells off enough does the equity go below the targeted buffer zone can also allow for outperformance capture. Generating a higher percentage in really good years can also help to offset losses or hedging costs if investors have multiple strategies in the portfolio. And there might be a place at the right allocation percentage for different strategies that all have varied risk profiles.

Figure 63. S&P 500 Index Total Return Annually 1928–2016.

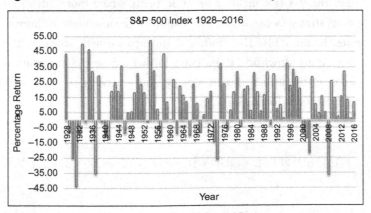

Data Source: Aswath Damodaran, NYU Stern School of Business.

Buffered strategies offer the ability to suspend a tranche of the downside but not all of it. During discussion on the Buffered Index Strategies with the portfolio managers, a great analogy came about that really describes the approach which had to do with wearing a seat belt. The idea was a seat belt generally provides a buffer against injury in accidents but if the accident is bad enough even a seat belt won't prevent every injury. But wearing the seat belt provides a cushion so if you're going to be driving anyway why not wear one? For those with equities in their pie charts, why not put the investing seat belt on instead?

The great thing about options is that they can be adjusted to create varied levels of upside and downside participation. While the leveraged buffered strategy has a certain risk profile, I use other versions when appropriate. An example of a standard buffered equity strategy is shown in Figure 64, which outlines a profit-and-loss chart compared to simply long S&P 500 Index.

As you can see the target equity downside buffer still is up to −25% but the maximum downside target loss is −10%. The difference in this version is the upside. Notice that this traces the S&P 500 but then starts to trail it a little bit. This is the tradeoff for the lower downside risk. This also contains short duration high yield as a base.

For the less risk inclined or in accounts where more advanced options strategies cannot be used, another version might be appropriate. In the ZBIG IRA Buffered Indexed Growth strategy, the target equity downside is reduced further while still targeting a portion of the upside. Figure 65 gives an overview of the profit-and-loss targets for the strategy.

10.8. BUFFERED EQUITY BENEFITS TO RISK-ADJUSTED RETURNS

As we will cover in the next chapter, one of the ways strategies and funds are evaluated is on a risk-adjusted returns. We'll get

Figure 64. ZEGA ZBIG Standard Equity P&L vs. S&P 500 Index.

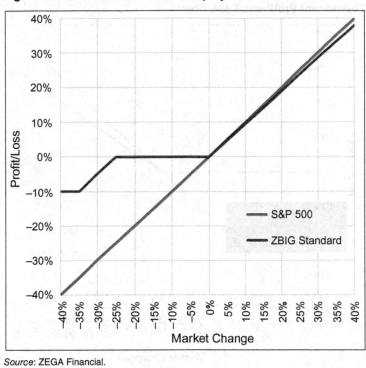

Source: ZEGA Financial.

into that more later, but typically popular ratios include standard deviation, returns, and some risk-free rate. In some, up and downside volatility can work against the measurements. In others, only downside returns count against the metrics. The reason buffered investments, in my opinion, may have some place in a more modern portfolio is simply giving investors the chance to avoid some of the bad stuff but still capturing the good can be a nice compliment to risk-adjusted returns.

These types of strategies are not just limited to large cap equities in the United States. If the goal is to reach emerging markets or developed equity in Europe, these same synthetic option frameworks along with a fixed income base enable buffered exposure

**Figure 65. ZBIG Buffered Indexed Growth IRA Equity
Component Profit-and-Loss Chart.**

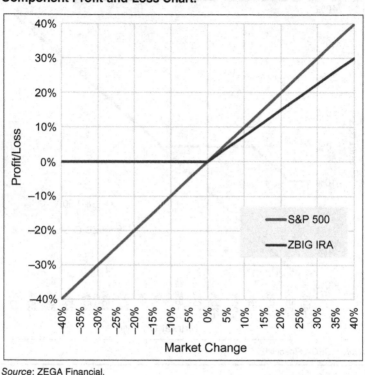

Source: ZEGA Financial.

there too. We had talked about target date funds and how they
adjusted to more of a fixed income allocation the closer one got
toward a retirement age. These Buffered Indexed Growth strategies
aim to have the volatility of a high yield fixed income profile. Plus,
the exchange-traded funds may be of the short duration where the
internal bonds are held to maturity. A bond held to maturity, provided there is no default, should return the par value back. This is
helpful since if the value of bonds should fluctuate, at some point
the idea is to get back to par.

Finally, the other nice aspect of the strategies is flexibility. If
markets should move too far in either direction since they are

liquid instruments, the strategy has the room to make adjustments. Like anything with investing, nothing is guaranteed. But looking to put the probabilities in the investors favor can help them achieve their retirement goals.

10.9. COVERED CALLS DO NOT CREATE SUBSTANTIAL HEDGES OR BUFFERS TO PORTFOLIOS

One area I wanted to address is the belief that selling covered calls offers material protection to portfolios or a true buffer against losses. Covered calls are the exercise of selling a short call against stock that you already own. The trade can also be put on simultaneously called a buy write. When you sell a short call, as the seller you are obligated to deliver shares at the strike price sold. It is considered covered because unlike a naked call, which would require the writer to go out into the open market and buy the shares at market, a covered call if exercised simply delivers the shares already in the account.

Over my years giving talks to investors, I can recount quite a few times when audience members would say they are hedging their positions using covered calls. Or the belief that the premium received from selling a covered call would create a real buffer. The reality is that the premium received from calls can add to a return, but generally they are not nearly high enough to offer the types of buffers described above. Consider the SPY exchange traded fund with a price of $247.50. If you go out a little over a year on the options chain and find a call option to sell roughly 10% higher in price, you would only generate about 1.2% return. And you just capped your upside by putting that ceiling on. Go up in price 20% higher and you would generate just 0.002%. The percentage gained from the sale of covered calls simply would not provide any downside protection or buffer. Considering markets have a historical standard deviation of annual returns of just over 19%, it is legitimate to think price can move above.

10.10. WHITE SWAN RISK

In the last chapter, we talked about Black Swan risk. But for covered call sellers there is a risk that they will cap their upside. Covered call strategies are often one of the first things learned by budding option investors. Part of the reason is they are easy to understand. The risk is missed profits for the most part instead of large drawdowns. Too often though the story goes like this. A covered call is written and probably too close to the current stock price. The reason being that in order to take in a good amount of premium, calls have to be sold closer to at-the-money. This has been especially the case in the lower volatility and interest rate environments since 2008–2009.

The underlying stock moves up through the covered call strike, thus capping profits and causing the investor to miss out on a nice run. They then spend the next year trying to roll the covered call out further in time and higher up, but the stock keeps running, thus continuing to miss out. Unlike Black Swan risk, which is thought to be unexpected and out of the blue, White Swan risk is clearly visible. Like the explorers who knew there were white swans all over, investors know that stocks can go up. Believe it or not, the market outdoes its historical standard deviation on the upside more often than you might think. Consider Figure 66, which shows the years the S&P 500 Index total return was greater than 20% over the 1928–2016 period.

Selling covered calls requires a bit more finesse than many realize. The option Greeks have to be analyzed and monitored to determine when to roll forward the contracts. Rolling is the process of buying the covered call to close and simultaneously selling a new covered call further out on the expiration curve. The management can be more time consuming than originally thought, and too often what is thought to be protection winds up being a headache as profits may be missed after being capped at inopportune areas.

The graph in Figure 66 showing how markets do outperform on the upside in many years is encouraging. Especially through the lens of some of the Buffered Indexed Strategies, which participate in most or more of that upside growth. Investors want to be able

Figure 66. S&P 500 Index Total Return Best Years 1928–2016.

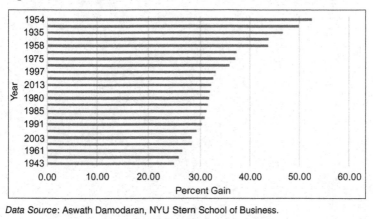

Data Source: Aswath Damodaran, NYU Stern School of Business.

to participate in that upside but just have a cushion. Investors do need growth, but they don't want to reach for it at the expense of having no downside protection. With options, so much more is possible. Moving forward, the pie chart can have exposure to equities but with shifted risk attributes.

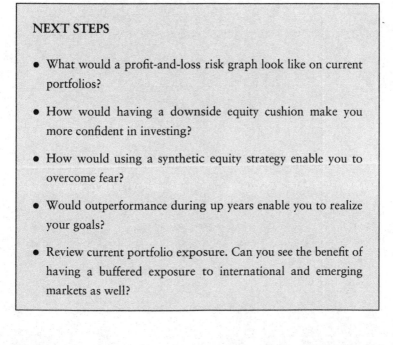

NEXT STEPS

- What would a profit-and-loss risk graph look like on current portfolios?

- How would having a downside equity cushion make you more confident in investing?

- How would using a synthetic equity strategy enable you to overcome fear?

- Would outperformance during up years enable you to realize your goals?

- Review current portfolio exposure. Can you see the benefit of having a buffered exposure to international and emerging markets as well?

11

RISK-ADJUSTED RETURNS MATTER

How many times have you heard a pundit on television say that a mutual fund or exchange-traded fund has beaten the S&P 500 Index over the last couple years? People become obsessed with whether they are beating an index. The comparisons are natural, given that it is easy to follow the general market. The problem is the S&P 500 Index is made up of large cap US equities. Sure, many companies have extensive exposure to foreign markets. But that is truly what that index represents. So, a strategy that also invests in, either through individual companies or funds, large cap stocks might compare how it did to a like comparison.

What does not make as much sense is investing in companies or funds in a specific area and then comparing that to the S&P 500 Index as its benchmark. If an investor holds a basket of New Zealand real estate companies, they hold an entirely different risk profile. If that basket did better than the S&P 500 Index that doesn't mean it beat a benchmark, as the S&P 500 would not be the appropriate yard stick. Instead, it just means that investing in New Zealand real estate stocks performed better as an asset class.

Active management has come under fire for not showing people returns greater than their respective indexes. During times of large positive correlation, passive indexing tends to be tougher to outperform. In periods of non-correlation, there is more of a difference. The fact remains though that too often people look at their investments as either doing better or worse than the major market indices and making determinations on success or failure based on that fact. Portfolios holding 60% Large Cap US Stocks and 40% US 10-Year Treasury bonds should not be compared to the S&P 500.

When we think about the intention of many portfolio-return evaluations, they are looking to figure out what type of movement did the investor experience to get where they are going? Having traveled quite a bit for work over the years gave me plenty of stories and analogies comparing air travel to investing. I can remember a time when I had to fly between Phoenix Arizona and Miami Florida twice in a month. The two flights couldn't have been more different. It was the same flight time, same flight number, same airline, and same plane type. The first flight was on-time and pretty unremarkable. Sort of a good thing for a plane flight. Ride was smooth as can be.

The next time I took the same flight we flew into afternoon thunderstorms it seemed like the whole way. I don't think the seatbelt sign was ever off and a good portion of the flight the crew was asked to be seated by the captain for their safety as we experienced a pretty good bit of turbulence the whole way. Both flights got us from point A to point B in the same amount of time but I would say we had quite a bit of volatility during the second flight. If there was a risk-adjusted airline flight ratio, the first one would have won out even though we go to the same place on both. This is the intention of formulas, in that they try to capture how crazy the ride was to get the investment returns that were provided.

11.1. RISK-ADJUSTED RETURNS

A better approach would be to evaluate how much the return has been relative to the risk. Have the returns generated aligned with what one needs to grow their assets before and in retirement? Have returns increased or decreased the probability of meeting goals for their assets? Of course, those within reach of retirement really do not want large swings or downside volatility in the value of their portfolios. Learning how to calculate not only your risk-adjusted return but also on potential investment strategies can help to filter out a lot of the noise. Learning to focus on the right things will lend itself to remaining focused on your goals and aspirations not what simply had the best returns over the last quarter.

If you asked most investors whether or not they would enjoy wild swings in the value of their investments, they probably would answer "No." The idea of having the highest return with the least amount of risk is the unicorn of investment strategies. The premise behind a risk-adjusted return is to quantify several factors that attempt to evaluate not which strategy returns the most percent gain over a period, but the best risk-adjusted return. Say one strategy has an average annualized return of 10% and another 12%. Without any other information, one might assume the strategy earning 12% to be better. But what if I told you that the standard deviation of the 10% return was 11% but the 12% return standard deviation was 20%? The latter strategy had experienced a much greater volatility in its returns. So, in theory, the first strategy, even at a lower annualized return, had a better risk-adjusted return.

In evaluating what risk was taken to produce returns, professionals have used a number of financial metrics looking to quantify performance. There are drawbacks. For example, just as we discussed about utilizing many years of historical returns to try to gauge future results, advanced risk analytics might only give investors an idea of how an approach has performed in the past. Long historical returns might not give investors with certainty what they might expect over the next shorter window of 10 years just before retirement. They also don't try to adjust for various interest rate environments. Not the risk-free rate, which we will discuss in a bit, but how high and low interest rates affect asset classes and future earnings. Despite the drawbacks, breaking down some ways to view a risk-adjusted return can help frame how your portfolio is tracking.

When looking at some popular ratios, many of them grab in some form or another the average return over a period, the standard deviation from the average, and a risk-free rate of return. The standard deviation is designed to tell us how far up or down something deviates from its mean or average.

As a reminder, the standard deviation measures how much the values vary in relation to its mean or average. The higher the standard deviation in returns, the more returns value higher or lower than the average and vice versa. The reason standard deviation is used alongside percentage returns is that it represents how much of a roller coaster ride an investor needed to endure to attain their return. If the ideal outcome is to get the most return with the least amount of volatility or risk, many market participants turn to ratios in order to look to determine what a strategies' risk-adjusted return is.

Think about the weather during the summer. If one town sees temperatures of 99 degree Fahrenheit one day and the next day 101, the sum of those two days is 200. The average temperature (200/2) would be 100 degrees. Its standard deviation would be 1. Now think about another town where they experienced the first day a reading of 80 degrees and the second day 120 degrees. Quite a bit of fluctuation compared to the first town. Yet the average temperature still saw the same sum of 200 and the average also the same of 100 degrees. The standard deviation was much higher, equal to 20. The second town experienced much greater volatility in temperature compared to the first.

If we visually look at the graphical comparison between Portfolio A and Portfolio B in Figure 67, we can see that one had more of a range of peaks and valleys than the other. One had much more volatility than the other. But, which one is better based upon a risk-adjusted return ratio?

To keep things simple as we explore some examples we will assume we are evaluating annual return numbers. Using weekly or monthly might require extra steps to annualize. In Table 22 we use

Figure 67. Comparing Two Portfolios' Visual Volatility of Annual Returns over 10 Years.

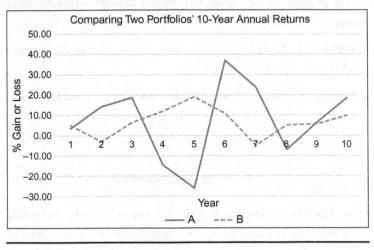

Table 22. Hypothetical Annual Returns over a 10-Year Period.

Year	Portfolio A Return	Portfolio B Return
1	3.56%	5.00%
2	14.22%	−3.00%
3	18.76%	6.54%
4	−14.31%	12.00%
5	−25.90%	19.03%
6	37.00%	11.00%
7	23.83%	−5.00%
8	−6.98%	5.20%
9	6.51%	5.70%
10	18.52%	10.00%

a 10-year stream of returns from the graph in Figure 67 to provide an example. By adding up the returns and dividing by the number of years, we can find an average annual return. Using Excel you can easily input this data and have it compute the average as well as the standard deviation. The years with a negative return are highlighted.

The average annual return and the standard deviation for these two portfolios are:

- Portfolio A: Average Annual Return 7.52%, Standard Deviation 18.02%

- Portfolio B: Average Annual Return 6.65%, Standard Deviation 6.68%

11.2. SHARPE RATIO

While Portfolio A has a higher average return, it also experienced more volatility as indicated by the standard deviation. One way to quantify which portfolio experienced a superior risk-adjusted return is to use a Sharpe Ratio. The higher the Sharpe Ratio, the higher the risk-adjusted return. When comparing multiple portfolios, the one with the highest Sharpe would be deemed, at least on the risk-adjusted scale, to be superior.

The Sharpe Ratio is a widely used measure to do exactly that. Its inputs include the percentage return, the standard deviation, and the risk-free rate of return. A good input for the risk-free rate of return is a 3-month US Government Treasury Bill. The reason why the risk-free rate is important is it represents the return an investor could receive without taking any risk. If an investment does not achieve a return over the risk-free rate then it would have little value as why take the extra risk.

US Government bonds are thought to be riskless, in theory, since they are backed by the full faith and credit of the US Government. That and the treasury could always increase the money supply. For our example, we will assume a 1% risk-free rate of return. If you were evaluating returns over actual returns or periods, it would be important to use historical risk-free rates of return or some sort of average over the periods covered.

To calculate the Sharpe Ratio, we need:

• Annualized Rate of Return

• Risk-Free Rate of Return

• Standard Deviation of Annual Return

Sharpe Ratio = $[(\text{Average Rate of Return} - \text{Risk-Free Rate})/\text{STD Dev}]$

Portfolio A $[(7.52\% - 1\%)/18.02\%] = 0.36$

Portfolio B $[(6.65\% - 1\%)/6.68\%] = 0.85$

Even though Portfolio B earned an average annual return of 0.87 percentage points less, because of the significantly less standard deviation, it produced the stronger risk-adjusted return according to the Sharpe Ratio. This type of calculation looks to not focus on just the absolute return and instead uses standard deviation, or large readings, as a proxy for risk. There are drawbacks, as it can only evaluate past performance; it might not take into account or anticipate potential risk not yet realized in a strategy. The other challenge with Sharpe is how it brings positive outsized returns into the model.

If we had a room of people with 10–15 years before retirement and asked how many would be alright with large losses, I imagine not many hands, if any, would go up in the room. Yet if we asked how many would love to see a huge gain in the next year that was greater than normal, every hand should go up except those who refuse to raise their hands no matter what the question is. If there were an outsized positive year, Sharpe would treat that increase in standard deviation on an up move the same as a down move. Thus the risk-adjusted return may wind up being lower unless the average return increased enough to overcome the increased standard deviation. In Table 23 we will use the same data points from the previous Portfolio B but instead add an 11th year with an annual return of +60%.

The average annual return jumps from 6.65% to 11.50%. The standard deviation also increases from 6.68% to 16.61%.

Table 23. Hypothetical Annual Returns Portfolio B over 10 and 11 Years.

Year	Portfolio B	Portfolio B.2
1	5.00%	5.00%
2	−3.00%	−3.00%
3	6.54%	6.54%
4	12.00%	12.00%
5	19.03%	19.03%
6	11.00%	11.00%
7	−5.00%	−5.00%
8	5.20%	5.20%
9	5.70%	5.70%
10	10.00%	10.00%
11		60.00%
AVG Annual Return	6.65%	11.50%
Standard Deviation	6.69%	16.61%
Sharpe Ratio	0.85	0.63

Remember our risk-adjusted return as determined by the Sharpe Ratio was 0.85.

Now this is interesting as the investor has more money in their investment portfolio and enjoyed a huge positive 60% return in year 11; however, the Sharpe Ratio now shifts lower to only 0.63 from 0.85, indicating that by adding that large extra upside result, the risk-adjusted return got worse. Most investors would probably welcome with open arms that type of year. There is, however, another ratio that looks to not penalize upside volatility above a pre-set minimum threshold a return has to achieve.

11.3. SORTINO RATIO

The Sortino Ratio differs from the Sharpe Ratio, in that a minimum acceptable return is set and anything below (worse) is counted in its standard deviation but returns at or above the minimum acceptable return are either not counted or set to zero. In this approach, upside outsized returns do not increase the standard deviation. By using only the downside deviation toward standard deviation it penalizes only those returns deemed to be unacceptable as well as the underperformance size below the acceptable return. We will look at both the original Portfolio B example and subsequent second example addition of an outsized upside return year to Portfolio B to understand how the Sortino Ratio is calculated and how it changes.

To calculate the Sortino Ratio we need the following:

• Average Annual Return

• Total Number of Return Periods

• Minimum Acceptable Return or MAR

• Underperformance from MAR Values

This calculation is a little more involved. The good news is that there are many online resources to assist in the effort and we will try to simplify it for you. Using an excel sheet is probably preferable as many of those formulas can be programmed into the cells. The formula, once you have done some number crunching, is:

$$\text{Sortino Ratio} = (\text{Average Return} - \text{Minimum Acceptable Return})/ \text{Downside Deviation}$$

A quick note on downside deviation. I use the returns below the minimum acceptable return and also include zero as the value for any return at or greater than the minimum acceptable return. More on that later, but I like doing it this way since it rewards less frequency of returns that fall short of the MAR.

The minimum acceptable return or MAR is a value or threshold that an investor would deem acceptable where any returns lower than that would underperform by a difference between the MAR and the return itself. This number is not pre-determined but rather chosen by the user. Some wanting to penalize only downside

deviation might choose a minimum return of 0% where any negative return would be counted. Returns that were acceptable would
either be thrown out and not used to compute the downside deviation or be assigned a value of zero.

Choosing only negative returns below zero would be a good
choice to keep things simple. In fact, we will use 0% in our examples. But others might choose something like the risk-free rate of
return as the threshold of acceptability. If one has deemed a neces-
sary return of say 4% then that could be the MAR value.

In Table 24 we have the 10-year Portfolio B and the 11-year
Portfolio B.2. In addition, we have listed the returns that were less
than the acceptable Minimum Average Return of 0%.

For any return that was 0% or greater, we just assign a value of
0% in that column. Also listed are the resulting figures from a few
steps needed to calculate the resulting Sortino Ratio for each portfolio. Again, Excel is going to be your friend on this one as there
are a few steps.

First, you will have calculated what the average annual return is
for each portfolio minus the target return. Since we have chosen
0%, this step is not as important had we chosen 4% or another
number. In that case you would take the average annual return −
MAR and then divide by the number of periods or years in our
example. Portfolio B had a 6.65% (average annual return − MAR)
while Portfolio B.2 settled at 11.50% after rounding up both.

Next if you look at the columns marked Ret < MAR, you will
want to square each of those and then total or sum. The SUMSQ
function in Excel allows you to easily do that and the resulting Sum
of Squares is listed in Table 24. They are the same for each portfolio
version because they both have the same down performance years.

Then you will want to take the average of all the squared
returns below MAR. Note that once you have the average, you
will want to divide that by the number of years. Since the first
return stream is for 10 years and the second is for 11 years, the
average sum of squares is different between the two calculations.
In this Sortino calculation, we do include the 0% values listed as

Table 24. Comparing Two Portfolios' Sortino Ratios.

	Portfolio B 10 Years		Portfolio B.2 11 Years	
Year	Ret	Ret < MAR	Ret	Ret < MAR
1	5.00%	0.00%	5.00%	0.00%
2	−3.00%	−3.00%	−3.00%	−3.00%
3	6.54%	0.00%	6.54%	0.00%
4	12.00%	0.00%	12.00%	0.00%
5	19.03%	0.00%	19.03%	0.00%
6	11.00%	0.00%	11.00%	0.00%
7	−5.00%	−5.00%	−5.00%	−5.00%
8	5.20%	0.00%	5.20%	0.00%
9	5.70%	0.00%	5.70%	0.00%
10	10.00%	0.00%	10.00%	0.00%
11			60.00%	0.00%
	Number	10		11
	Sum of Squares	0.0034		0.0034
	AVG SUM SQs	0.00034		0.000309
	SQRT AVG Sum SQ	0.018439		0.017581
	Sortino Ratio	3.605127		6.541159

well as any downside negative returns. None of the years are excluded.

This is also listed in the table. Then take the square root of that result. Finally, the last step is to take the average annual return above MAR and divide by the square root of the average of the sum of squares.

The first Portfolio B achieved a Sortino Ratio of 3.61 while Portfolio B.2 had a higher, and thus better, 6.54 ratio. After all those steps, you might have forgotten that in the Sharpe Ratio calculation when we added the 11th year of a +60% return, the Sharpe Ratio went down even though the return was an outsized-up year. This was because even extremely positive returns are included in the standard deviation calculation. With only using returns that deviated from the minimum acceptable return and assigning a 0% to others, this did not hold upside deviations as a negative. Most investors would be just fine with as much upside volatility and positive deviation from the average compared with downside. Reducing downside or limiting their size can have long-term positive effects on portfolios.

A quick note around the calculation of the Sortino Ratio. I've been asked a couple times when presenting in front of large groups whether to just use, and thus average, only the downside deviation periods, or use both downside deviation amounts and years where return was above MAR threshold. In that case, as we did above, a value of 0% would be assigned. The reason why I include all of the periods is simply if you include the returns which are above MAR with the ones that fall below, this rewards lower frequency of downside return periods. When calculating these ratios and comparing one strategy to another, it will be important to utilize the same methodology so an apples-to-apples comparison can be made.

Remember, these types of ratios can input historical data and evaluate what has happened. They may help to understand what is probable but not certain in a future period. Strategies without enough history may not fully reflect the potential risk. Of course, these also cannot predict fully the potential for outsized unforeseen returns. But the reason to go into the methodology of a risk-adjusted return and understand what would help and hurt these ratios is constructive in understanding what investors can try and control in portfolios. Some strategies that have years in a row without a loss might not reveal their downside risk in such ratios. In that regard, they do have some drawbacks.

Unfortunately, too often the fallback is to continuously just compare against the entire market and to judge a strategy on whether or not it beats or underperforms. The whole story is so much more. What also is challenging is using many years of historical returns to build a portfolio for someone with much less time. The traditional asset allocation into the standard pie charts leans too heavily on historical averages as some expectation of the future. With regard to bonds, outside of the last 9 years, interest rates were much higher and had been falling for over 35 years.

If we identify what can increase or decrease something like a Sortino Ratio, what are some things that could be done to build a new, more updated pie chart focused on a more person goal-oriented approach — one that understands many investors might only have smaller windows to grow and protect assets in order to generate the required lifestyle in retirement?

In the end, maybe the goal for investors should be to work not to simply produce the highest return but instead to manage the things that will increase your risk-adjusted return ratio. Focus on the process instead of the outcomes and the outcome will resolve itself. Using traditional metrics that punish upside positive results would seem to not be in alignment with what a typical investor would want.

So, as we look at strategies which can help focus on the process not the outcome, believing the outcome will resolve itself, what can we do in order to start building portfolios using new information? The Sortino Ratio is helped by larger returns above a minimum acceptable return. Larger returns are good, right? Many in the home stretch of building for retirement may still need more growth to ensure they have what they need from an asset base and future income. More than likely to increase that chance, you need equity exposure. The challenge with a normal equity slice in the portfolio is the potential for 2008-like losses. Large downside deviations from the MAR would hurt a Sortino Ratio.

So, if an investor wanted to decrease the probability of a sizeable loss or number of losses going forward, it would seem like strategies which either hedge the downside or buffer it make sense. Think about the ability to still capture most of the upside but put a hard floor for the downside. If you could cap losses to an acceptable level while generating upside when markets ran, wouldn't that help your portfolio's risk-adjusted return?

Traditional asset allocation that builds the typical age-specific blend between stocks and bonds usually follow some sort of glide path like we explored during our discussion on the target date funds. The reason why adjustments are made to move toward more and more fixed income, the closer an investor gets to retirement, is that bonds have had less total volatility, both up and down, historically. But when we think back about the rough periods for those close to retirement in target date funds, they were designed in the hope that over a shorter period they would produce a return more like the long-term average. Unfortunately, that may not be the case.

The reason to go in to the idea of risk-adjusted returns and to illustrate how two of them work should give investors a good idea of how the inputs that are created via volatility and returns can have both positive and negative effects on their portfolios. It also shows why just benchmarking against an index and adding money to or pulling money from investments based on simply beating or missing the index returns may not provide much value.

There is not a perfect metric or ratio that can predict every risk in a portfolio or investment. They certainly can't always predict the future. The work that people did to create these, especially considering many of these were worked through before the benefit of computers or excel spreadsheets, is impressive. Often questions come up about what a good Sharpe or Sortino Ratio is? With the Sharpe Ratio, the higher the result, the better. Sometime people point to a level greater than 1 as good and above 1.5 great. Other people might dismiss the idea of whether a strategy has a high number and rather would simply use a ratio to compare like strategies as a comparison tool. So, what have historical markets produced in terms of a Sharpe Ratio, for example?

11.4. HISTORICAL SHARPE RATIOS: EQUITIES AND UNITED STATES TREASURIES

As we learned above we need an average annual return, a standard deviation of those returns, and a risk-free rate in the case of a Sharpe Ratio. Figure 68 shows the average annual rate for the continuous maturity 3-Month Treasury Bill.

In the figure we have an annual average for each year from 1934 to 2015. The question about what to use for a risk-free rate is often asked. I tend to just use a 3-Month United States Treasury Bill but sometimes people might use the 1-Year United States Treasury or short-term commercial paper. Since the time frame for annual returns started in 1928, when calculating a Sharpe Ratio, I used the New York 6-Month commercial paper annualized rate for 1928 through 1933. Using this method to generate an average annual risk-free rate, we come up with 3.53%. Imagine the

Figure 68. 3-Month Treasury Bill Continuous Maturity Average Annual Rate 1934–2016.

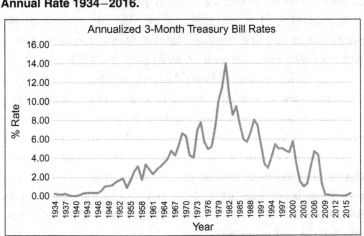

Data Source: Board of Governors of the Federal Reserve System and Federal Reserve Bank St. Louis.

**Table 25. Portfolio Sharpe Ratio 1928–2016 with 3.53%
Risk-Free Rate.**

Market	Sharpe Ratio
S&P 500 Index Total Return	0.40
10-Year US Treasury Bonds	0.21
70/30 S&P 500 Total Return & 10 Year US TR	0.42
60/40 S&P 500 Total Return & 10 Year US TR	0.42
50/50 S&P 500 Total Return & 10 Year US TR	0.43
40/60 S&P 500 Total Return & 10 Year US TR	0.42
30/70 S&P 500 Total Return & 10 Year US TR	0.41
20/80 S&P 500 Total Return & 10 Year US TR	0.37

Data Source: Board of Governors of the Federal Reserve System, Federal Reserve
Bank St. Louis, and Aswath Damodaran NYU Stern School of Business.

---

risk-free rate in 1981 was around 14%, which means that an investment in that year would really have to work hard in order to create a Sharpe Ratio that was actually positive.

We examine the Sharpe Ratio on the total return of the S&P 500 Index, the 10-Year United States Treasury, and a blended 60/40 equities/treasuries, as displayed in Table 25.

What is interesting is how close all of these are taking a long-term view of annual returns. Like we said, nothing is perfect and they only look backwards and attempt to give some predictive nature to future risk-adjusted returns. Even using many years of returns might not recognize some structural change. For example, interest rates were quite a bit higher than they have been since 2008. Real risk evaluation must still be done on portfolios to understand whether or not it is the right mix for the end investor.

NEXT STEPS

- Outline what you require to meet your goals before and after retirement.

- Take an inventory of current investments to evaluate their risk-adjusted returns and downside deviation.

- Consider strategies that can mitigate downside deviation through hedging or buffers.

- Evaluate whether your current portfolio's process will lead to more positive than negative inputs to the Sortino Ratio.

- What steps with your current investments could you take in order to limit large drawdowns?

12

FINAL THOUGHTS

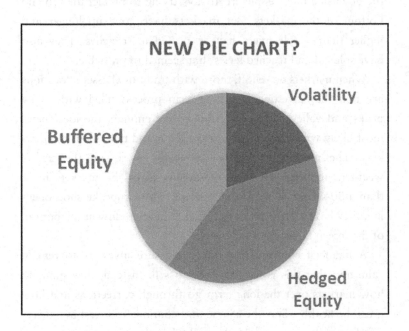

NEW PIE CHART?

Volatility

Buffered
Equity

Hedged
Equity

What will be in your updated pie chart? Will it be the same as it has been for years or something new? Maybe it will resemble the pie chart above? The percentages for an investor would be specific to them, but hedged equity, buffered equity, and volatility may find a place in an updated portfolio.

Throughout the course of the book, we examined the traditional portfolios and their historical averages. We discussed the challenge with using long-term averages to make assumptions about the next decade or so. Moving forward, the case for bonds in portfolios becomes a bit cloudy as real returns will likely be sub-par if rates remain low. If rates rise, bond values get hit. We've seen that subtracting out the coupon payments from long-term historical returns tends to leave next to nothing left.

Rather than trying to call the next downturn or recession, it's about being ready. Ready to capitalize on the upside but minimize the downside risk. People are always trying to predict the top and bottom of the markets. But markets have gone up longer and higher than people might have expected in stretches. They also have sold off and reached levels that seemed improbable.

When markets do selloff, those with traditional asset allocations are told that investing is a long-term process filled with many peaks and valleys. If a correction is bad enough, the local news most likely will find someone to come on and talk about the markets. The morning news that typically gives you the traffic, weather, and regional stories suddenly gives the markets more than a 30-second spot. While covering a new cupcake shop opening, they have a Dow Jones price ticker in a window at the bottom of the screen throughout the show.

A financial expert comes on to reassure investors to remain calm and that this is not the time to sell. Instead, they point to how markets over the long term go through corrections and how it can be healthy. Stay the course and continue to invest in a diversified portfolio. They might also talk about making sure you aren't 100% in equities and to make sure and have a mix of stocks and bonds to lessen the downside risk. They may even throw out the old formula of taking your 100 minus your age to come up with what percent can be invested in stocks. Remember what happened to many target date funds that did use by their models and age-appropriate traditional allocation.

Whenever I see a scenario like the one above, I believe people shouldn't just be told to accept that everything is going to be just fine doing things the way we've always done it. Of course, they shouldn't panic and make rash decisions. But days like that should be a wakeup call. Rather than just quoting the same script, investors should take the opportunity to think about whether they want to add true protection to their portfolios. What are you going to do in order to protect and grow the assets to try and achieve investment goals? What is your time horizon instead of thinking about averages over a hundred years?

During the 2008 downturn, I saw various people go on local and national news trying to explain what was going on. At various stages of the downturn, I heard all the same things. Markets have sold off so much already, it would be unprecedented to keep going lower. Eventually they did. They talked about the diversification thing. How maintaining a proper asset allocation that diversified portfolios between sectors and asset classes will contain losses. They didn't as most things became highly correlated.

The issue for many investors is that portfolios designed to work in the long term didn't for those with short time frames to retirement. Take the target date funds we explored with retirement year of 2010 during the crisis. They had severe drawdowns that shocked many investors. As I've maintained, the target date funds never guaranteed against downside losses. Instead, they just switched their allocation to more bonds. If downside protection is really what these close to retirees wanted, why not use hedged equity instead?

In the aftermath of 2008, and even to this day, I continue to see investors that sold at the worst time and remained underinvested, or in cash positions thus missing out on the rebound. That type of fear is natural. True hedging involves being in strategies that can mitigate the downside through positions that avoid risk below a certain threshold. Imagine having real hedges not soft floors in portfolios during this time. One of the attributes of well-constructed hedging strategies is after avoiding the majority of downturns, investors will purchase more of the market at lower levels using any hedging profits or avoided losses.

We explored the idea of the buffered growth strategies that provide a cushion should markets retract to a certain level yet still capture more of the upside in the most aggressive form. The good news is equity markets on average finish positive in most years. In some years, they outperform compared to probability of a certain return in a given year. These synthetic positions contain equity-like characteristics but a shifted profit-and-loss graph. At the same time, they utilize risk substitution where the core of the portfolio is in less volatile fixed income.

Short volatility on a smaller percentage of the portfolio offers an alternative income strategy that is not simply dependent on the markets going higher. Post 2008 we started to see Black Swan protection funds crop up, which would put very far out-of-the-money put options. Since long volatility on markets tends to erode balances over time, it is no surprise that funds have consistently lost money. The cost of owning one of these to create a proportional position to equities would seem quite high. Over time, while with its own risk set, it has been shown to be a higher probability to sell volatility on very far away options than owning them. If you think about paying your car insurance bill each month over many years, you will have paid in much more than your current car is worth.

As we move forward into the next decade, markets may not behave like they have in the past. In the next 10-year period, the returns for the fixed income asset class might be looked at as one of the more challenging periods. Why not try new approaches and strategies? What remains interesting is that if producing the best risk-adjusted return is mentioned as the reason to still go with some classic asset allocation, why is the very measure (Sharpe Ratio) so low?

My hope is that not only will investors have access to and utilize alternative approaches, but that the financial community embraces new ideas and and engage in a debate.

BIBLIOGRAPHY

Bank of England. (2016). Retrieved from https://www.bankofengland.co.uk/monetarypolicy/decisions.htm

Bary. (2014). Retrieved from http://www.barrons.com/articles/target-date-funds-take-over-1404460045?mg=prod/accounts-barrons

Blinder & Zandi. (2010). Retrieved from http://www.imf.org/external/pubs/ft/fandd/2010/12/Blinder.htm

Braham. (2013). Retrieved from https://www.bloomberg.com/news/2013-01-18/a-devil-s-bargain-faces-investors-in-popular-structured-notes.html

Brigham & Ehrhardt. (2014). *Financial management: Theory and practice* (14th ed.).

Buffett & Loomis. (2001). Retrieved from http://archive.fortune.com/magazines/fortune/fortune_archive/2001/12/10/314691/index.htm

Businessinsider.com. (2016). Retrieved from http://www.businessinsider.com/every-stock-market-crash-in-past-60-years-2016-6

CBOE.COM. (2017). Retrieved from http://www.cboe.com/blogs/options-hub/2017/03/01/eight-charts-highlighting-growth-in-options-and-vix-futures

CNN.Money.com. (2005). Retrieved from http://money.cnn.com/2005/12/27/news/economy/inverted_yield_curve/index.htm

Damodaran. (2016). Retrieved from http://pages.stern.nyu.edu/
~adamodar/ (cited in both text and graphs/tables)

Federal Reserve. (2017). Retrieved from https://www.federalre-
serve.gov/releases/h41/current/h41.htm#h41tab9

Federal Reserve Bank of Atlanta. (2017). Retrieved from https://
www.frbatlanta.org/chcs/wage-growth-tracker.aspx?panel=1

FRED. Retrieved from https://fred.stlouisfed.org/series/
ECBASSETS

FRED. World Bank, Life Expectancy at Birth, Total for the United
States [SPDYNLE00INUSA]. FRED, Federal Reserve Bank of
St. Louis. Retrieved from https://fred.stlouisfed.org/series/
SPDYNLE00INUSA. Accessed on July 28, 2017.

Furth. (2013). Retrieved from http://www.heritage.org/debt/report/
high-debt-real-drag#_ftnref3

Gallup. (2014). Retrieved from http://news.gallup.com/poll/
168626/retirement-remains-americans-top-financial-worry.aspx

GPO.gov. (2009). Retrieved from https://www.gpo.gov/fdsys/pkg/
CPRT-111SPRT53067/pdf/CPRT-111SPRT53067.pdf

Hale. (2017). Retrieved from http://www.cbsnews.com/news/
oppenheimers-bond-fund-blowup-worse-than-you-think/

KFF.Org. (2014). Retrieved from http://www.kff.org/other/state-
indicator/avg-annual-growth-per-capita/?currentTimeframe=0&
sortModel=%7B%22colId%22:%22Location%22,%22sort%22:
%22asc%22%7D

McDonald. (2013). Retrieved from http://fortune.com/2012/03/12/
meredith-whitney-was-right/

Meisler. (2017). Retrieved from https://www.bloomberg.com/
graphics/2017-state-pension-funding-ratios/

National Bureau of Economic Research. Retrieved from http://
www.nber.org/cycles.html (table).

NOAA.gov. (n.d.). Retrieved from http://www.lightningsafety.
noaa.gov/odds.shtml

OMB. (2017). Retrieved from https://www.whitehouse.gov/omb/
budget/Historicals

Retirement Funds Glidepath. Retrieved from https://www4.trowe-
price.com/iws/wps/wcm/connect/cb07f2804dc1463caf7dbf2f8c725
be8/RetirementFunds_Glidepath_HardCard.pdf?MOD=AJPERES&
CACHEID=cb07f2804dc1463caf7dbf2f8c725be8

Reuters. Retrieved from http://www.reuters.com/article/us-japan-
boj-balancesheet-idUSKBN18T04D

SEC.GOV. (2010). Retrieved from https://www.sec.gov/news/
press/2010/2010-103.htm

Statista.com. (n.d.). Retrieved from https://www.statista.com/
statistics/224579/worldwide-etf-assets-under-management-since-
1997/

Steyer. (2014). Retrieved from http://www.pionline.com/article/
20141124/ONLINE/141129936/cerulli-target-date-funds-snag-
ging-larger-share-of-401k-assets

Templeton. (2009). Retrieved from https://seekingalpha.com/arti-
cle/112934-dow-dogs-were-dogs-in-2008-what-about-2009

uky.edu. (n.d.). Retrieved from http://www.uky.edu/~dsianita/
695ec/failure.html

WSJ.COM. (2011). Retrieved from http://www.wsj.com/video/
cuban-on-investing-diversification-is-for-idiots/233AE43E-9DA3-
40A3-8F6B-9DC23DD82BEF.html

WSJ.COM. (2017). Retrieved from https://blogs.wsj.com/econom-
ics/2017/05/19/how-cell-phone-plans-with-unlimited-data-limited-
inflation/

Ycharts. (2016). Retrieved from https://ycharts.com/indicators/
sandp_500_dividend_yield_ttm/chart/#/?securities=id:I:SP500DYT,
include:true,,&calcs=&correlations=&zoom=3&startDate=&
endDate=&format=real&recessions=false&chartView=&
chartType=interactive&splitType=single&scaleType=linear&
securitylistName=&securitylistSecurityId=&securityGroup=&
displayTicker=false&title=&note=&units=false&source=false&
liveData=false&quoteLegend=true&legendOnChart=true&part-
ner=basic_850&useEstimates=false

INDEX